# INVASION
# THE STORY OF
# D-DAY

## • BRUCE BLIVEN JR. •

young
voyageur

For

Allen, David, Douglas,
Eric, Joey, Keith,
Mark, Peter, Terry, Tom,
Tony, and Wallace

Brimming with creative inspiration, how-to projects, and useful information to enrich your everyday life, Quarto Knows is a favorite destination for those pursuing their interests and passions. Visit our site and dig deeper with our books into your area of interest: Quarto Creates, Quarto Cooks, Quarto Homes, Quarto Lives, Quarto Drives, Quarto Explores, Quarto Gifts, or Quarto Kids.

Inspiring | Educating | Creating | Entertaining

© 2017 Quarto Publishing Group USA Inc.
Original text © 1956 Bruce Bliven, Jr.
Additional material © 2007 Flying Point Press, © 2017 Quarto Publishing Group USA Inc.

First published in 1956 by Random House. This edition published in 2017 by Voyageur Press, an imprint of The Quarto Group, 401 Second Avenue North, Suite 310, Minneapolis, MN 55401 USA. Telephone: (612) 344-8100 Fax: (612) 344-8692

QuartoKnows.com

Voyageur Press titles are also available at discount for retail, wholesale, promotional, and bulk purchase. For details, contact the Special Sales Manager by email at specialsales@quarto.com or by mail at The Quarto Group, Attn: Special Sales Manager, 401 Second Avenue North, Suite 310, Minneapolis, MN 55401 USA.

10 9 8 7 6 5 4 3 2 1

ISBN: 978-0-7603-5436-0

Library of Congress Control Number: 2017933046

Series Design: Beth Middleworth
Series Creative Director: Laura Drew
Page Layout: Beth Middleworth

On the front cover: *Getty Images*
On the back cover: *Library of Congress*

Printed in China

# CONTENTS

# CHAPTER ONE

# THE GREAT ASSAULT

The end of World War II began on June 6, 1944.

That was the day American, British, and Canadian troops, who had sailed across the Channel from England, invaded the continent of Europe. They attacked a fifty-mile strip of the coast of Normandy in German-held France.

It was the greatest amphibious (water-borne) assault in the history of warfare.

If you talk about "D-Day," most people assume that this is the D-Day you mean, although the term is used by the Army to mean the day of any

Adolf Hitler saluting a parade of the SS troops, circa 1938.

attack. June 6, 1944, outranks all the other D-Days there have been, and the chances are that the world will never again see an amphibious assault on such a huge scale. In the future, no one is going to think what the German dictator, Adolf Hitler, thought: that the whole coast of a continent can be defended by building a concrete and barbed-wire barrier along its seashore. The growth of air power and the development of guided and ballistic missiles have made Hitler's idea ridiculous.

It wasn't ridiculous in 1944. At that time, the use of airborne troops who dropped to the battlefield in parachutes and gliders, and who could fly over fortifications, was brand new. Parts of three airborne divisions were used in the Normandy assault, but theirs was an assisting job. They delivered the first jab. The main effort—the knockout punch—was to be made by six divisions of infantrymen who traveled to the battlefield by boat.

It was against just such a seaborne invasion that Hitler had built his defensive line, his "Atlantic Wall," as he called it. The coastline of Europe had been fortified, foot by foot, all the way from Denmark down to the southern end of France. It wasn't really a wall. It was a network of obstacles placed in the water to rip the bottoms out of small boats and, on land, mines, pillboxes, forts, gun emplacements, and machine-gun nests, connected by trenches and protected by barbed wire barriers. Hitler thought it was strong enough to stop any invasion force. The Allies (as the Americans, British, and Canadians were called) agreed that the Atlantic Wall was very strong.

A sketch by Victor Lundy, who went on to become a successful architect and whose work includes the United States Tax Court Building in Washington, DC. During World War II, he enlisted in the Army, and filled up over two dozen sketchbooks with drawings of his time in the war in Europe. This sketch shows part of the Atlantic Wall, and the obstacles the Allies needed to overcome in order to re-take France.

Bird's-eye view of landing craft, barrage balloons, and Allied troops landing in Normandy, France, on D-Day.

No matter how many men take part in a landing, some few must be the first ashore.

They lead the way for all the others to follow.

Those who land first have a peculiarly tough job. In the minutes while they are leaving their boats and wading ashore, they are exposed and almost helpless. If the enemy is alert and ready to defend its shore, crossing the beach is another difficult time for the invaders. Beaches are generally flat and open, with no shelter from bullets. About the best an assault force can do is to get across a beach fast.

And then the first men ashore have to be supplied, quickly, with supporting weapons more powerful than the rifles, light machine guns, and light mortars they can carry with them.

The assault troops must seize a fairly large piece of ground in a hurry and build up strength within that beachhead. Until they do, even a small defending force may be able to drive the invaders back into the sea. So the early hours of an amphibious assault, even under the best of circumstances, are a gamble.

Hitler believed that his army, protected by its fortifications and blazing away with a variety of weapons, would be able to stop the Allies at, or close to, the water's edge.

He believed the Germans could smash the great assault before it really got going.

The Allies thought differently. They hoped their first few soldiers ashore would break through the beach fortifications and proceed far enough inland on D-Day to establish the first toehold in Europe. And that then the great weight of the combined armies, pouring through the small opening in the Atlantic Wall, could go on to win the war against Germany.

The question was: Could the leading assault troops break open the first holes in Hitler's defensive line?

That was what the soldiers themselves, before the end of D-Day, would answer. The success of the invasion depended on them.

· CHAPTER TWO ·

# ATTACK BY SECTION

There were more than 2.8 million men in the Allied expeditionary force. Of these, only a few thousand were going to lead the landings. And at around two o'clock on the morning of D-Day they were about ten miles from the French coast.

Most of them were aboard the large transports on which they had crossed the Channel.

Now they began to load into the small landing craft used for the actual attack.

The night was dark and rather cold.

Every man was nervous, even though the Germans, so far, had done nothing to show they knew what was coming.

Flamethrowers like this one were one of many types of ammunition carried ashore by the Allies. They sprayed slightly jellied gasoline, which would burn wherever it landed.

There were some reassuring ideas with which a soldier could face the job ahead. The first-wave infantrymen knew that they were going to get help from thousands of specialists—soldiers, sailors, and airmen—who had been carefully rehearsed in various assisting jobs. That was a comforting thought.

And it was possible, the assault troops felt, that if everything worked according to plan, the landings might be fairly easy.

But those who were veterans of other, earlier, landings knew that in an amphibious assault the plans never work perfectly.

Some of the men were not so much afraid as tense from days of waiting for D-Day to come. The suspense had mounted by the hour.

And so, for some of them, the order to load into the landing craft came as a kind of relief.

The assault boats were called LCVPs—initials that stood for Landing Craft, Vehicle, Personnel. They were the smallest of the many different kinds of landing craft that had been designed by the Allies during World War II. They were built to run right onto the shore—or, at least, into quite shallow water—where their square bows could be lowered, like small drawbridges, to become unloading ramps.

An LCVP could carry thirty-two men, and a thirty-two-man section was the basic unit, or team, in the attack.

The infantrymen got into their LCVPs by climbing over the rails and down the sides of the transport ships, using huge

## LIVING COSTS IN 1944

You may have talked to relatives who remember the days of World War II, or you may have heard stories about relatives who actually fought in the war. To get a better sense of the time period, take a look at the costs of common items in 1944:

Average annual wages: $2,400
Average cost of new house: $3,450
Average cost for house rent: $50 per month
Gallon of gas: 15 cents
Loaf of bread: 10 cents
First class postage stamp: 2 cents
Two dozen oranges: 33 cents

rope cargo nets as ladders. They had practiced this maneuver repeatedly during their training in England. It was not easy to do in the dark, carrying heavy and awkward equipment, and with the boats waiting at the bottom of the nets tossing in the choppy water. Both the wind and the waves were higher than the Allies had hoped they would be. But, on the whole, the loading of the small boats went well.

There were no seats in the LCVPs. The men took positions in the bargelike interiors of the boats in, roughly, three rows. Those in front would be the first to rush ashore. It was too crowded for everyone to sit at the same time, so the soldiers took turns standing, squatting, or sitting. The water was much too rough for comfort in any position. As the LCVPs loaded up and pulled away from the big transports, they began to rock and pitch. Waves slapped them, sending cold spray flying through the air. Before long everybody was soaked to the skin.

Each boat section carried terrific power. The men knew it and the knowledge was one of the things that gave them confidence.

A typical boatload in the first wave of the assault carried, first of all, standing in the bow, the boat section leader (a junior officer) with five riflemen. The riflemen carried semiautomatic Garand rifles (called M-1s) and each had ninety-six bullets in clips of eight with him. He wore the extra clips in pouches on the wide web belt around his waist. Tied to the suspenders that helped support his belt were some of the five hand grenades and four smoke grenades he carried. In addition, in one of the big pockets in his special assault jacket, he had a half-pound block of TNT and the fuse to set it off.

Next came four men, also armed with rifles, who made up a special wire-cutting team. Their job was to open gaps through barbed wire with the big cutters they carried.

Behind them were two Browning Automatic Rifle teams with two men to a team. A BAR, as the gun was called, is more like a machine gun than a rifle; it sprays lead around in rapid fire. Each team carried nine hundred rounds of ammunition.

Then came two men with bazookas, the amazing weapon which looks like a length of stovepipe and fires a small, bomblike rocket. Its range is only a few hundred yards, but when it hits, the rocket not only explodes with great force, but can burn its way through thin steel plate. Each bazooka man had an assistant to load the device and carry the extra rockets. He was armed with a carbine, a light rifle.

A four-man light mortar team came next. They carried a 60-millimeter mortar (whose barrel is a shade more than 2⅓ inches wide) and twenty mortar shells. Many of the men thought that the mortar was the infantry's most effective weapon. It is a tubular device that lobs its shell high into the air, so that it can reach over walls or hills.

It is accurate. And, when the shell explodes, it shatters into thousands of fragments that zip off in every direction with the force of bullets. Anyone standing near the place where a mortar shell goes off is almost sure to be hit.

A flamethrower team of two men followed the mortar section. Their flamethrower spurted slightly jellied gasoline through the air. It was set on fire as it left the nozzle and burned furiously for some little time after it hit. The flamethrowers were to be used against the concrete pillboxes and gun emplacements in the German fortifications. The team was to spray a pillbox with burning jelly to keep the men inside the pillbox from shooting, at least until the fire burned out.

During that time, the last section in the boat, the demolitions team of five men, was to perform its special job— perhaps the most daring of all. The demolitions men carried TNT. Some of it was in squarish packages called "satchel" charges. Some was lashed on the ends of poles perhaps ten feet long. The demolitions men were to advance all the way across the beach and plant their TNT against the concrete walls of the German pillboxes, or gun emplacements, or whatever the strongpoint in their particular section of the beach might be. They counted on the rifle, mortar, bazooka, and BAR teams to keep the Germans in the strongpoint fully occupied during their advance. They counted on the flamethrowers, immediately before the planting of the TNT, to douse the strongpoint with fire. Then, while the Germans were at least temporarily stunned by the violent attack, the demolitions men were to make their final rush. They were to set down the TNT wherever it would do the most damage, pull the gadget that set off the fuse, and, in a few seconds' time, hurl themselves back out of the way of the blast. The

TNT, if properly placed, could blow up almost any pillbox.

The assistant section leader, second in command, brought up the rear. He had with him one or two medical-aid men with first-aid supplies, who wore big red crosses painted on their helmets for easy identification.

There were six such boat sections—a total of about 192 men—in each assault infantry company.

And each of the first-wave companies was to attack a piece approximately 1,000 yards wide of one of the five main beaches.

The five beaches had code names. From west to east, in order, they were called Utah (where Americans were to land), Omaha (Americans), Gold (British), Juno (Canadians), and Sword (British).

When you hear that there were six divisions (90,000 men) in the attack, plus reinforcements of a dozen different kinds, it sounds like a great many men.

But looking at only the first wave of assault infantrymen, who had to start the actual attack on the beach defenses, it seemed like very few indeed.

On Omaha, for example, the first wave of troops was made up of only eight infantry companies—forty-eight boat sections containing a total of 1,536 soldiers. And Omaha, because it was in many ways the most important beach of all, had two divisions assigned to it. The 28,500 men in those two divisions waited to follow in the footsteps of the first 1,536 soldiers.

* * *

While the first-wave assault boats, fully loaded, waited for a signal to start their ten-mile run in to the beaches, they

An American soldier compares a German bazooka, nicknamed the *Panzerschreck* ("tank terror"), on the left, with an American 2.36-inch M1A1 bazooka on the right.

circled in groups, plowing through the choppy sea after each other like circus horses in a big ring.

H-Hour (which stands for the minute of an attack in the same way that D-Day stands for its date) had been set at 6:30 for both the American beaches, Utah and Omaha.

At 4:30 a.m. the LCVPs got the order to go.

The circles of boats straightened out into lines, with small navy guide boats leading the way. The lines moved toward the beaches.

As soon as the run began, many of the boat sections found themselves in what seemed like minor trouble. The spray, which had soaked everybody from the start, got heavier. Some LCVPs were filling with water and needed to run their automatic pumps at top speed. In a few cases even that was not enough. The infantrymen had to take off their helmets and use them to bail. This was unfortunate because it wasted strength that the soldiers would need later. Nor was that all. Despite the anti-seasickness pills they had been taking, the men got sick—not just a few of those with the weakest stomachs, but most of the men. Some, of course, were much sicker than others, but even a slight attack of seasickness is exhausting. The combination of wet cold, seasickness, and the cramped conditions in the heavily loaded LCVPs was discouraging.

On the other hand, the noise of the bombardment of the shore cheered the men up.

All fifty miles of coast were getting a tremendous pounding. It had started at 3:15, when more than 1,100 Royal Air Force bombers had blasted the invasion area with nearly 6,000 tons of bombs. And just half an hour before the landings, 1,365 heavy bombers of the United States Eighth Air Force were to drop another 3,000 tons of high explosives on Hitler's Atlantic Wall. They were 100-pound bombs for the most part, but with some 500-pound blockbusters mixed in for the biggest strongpoints. And fifteen minutes before the attack, medium-bombers and fighter-bombers of the United States Ninth Air Force would sweep the whole coast, paying special attention to the most troublesome German gun positions.

That was by no means all.

The guns of both the British and American navies were pummeling the coast. More than 700 of the 6,000 ships in the giant flotilla that had been assembled for D-Day were there to serve as floating artillery. They ranged in size from huge battleships such as the *Texas,* the *Arkansas,* the *Warspite,* and the *Ramillies,* whose biggest guns could throw their shells as far as seventeen miles, down to rocket-launching boats, hardly larger than the LCVPs. These rocket-launching boats were to fire clusters of high-explosive, self-propelling shells over the heads of the assault troops at the last safe moment—when they were just 300 yards from the beach. Each rocket boat was to drop 1,000 rockets on the beach in a few minutes' time. There were cruisers and destroyers with thousands of shells to fire. Tanks and self-propelled armored field-artillery guns were to blast away at the beach from the landing craft that had carried them across the Channel. Then they were to follow the first wave of troops ashore.

There had never been a bombardment anywhere of

such size and intensity. The total weight of high explosive dropped on the Normandy coast that morning was almost incredible. The plan was to "drench" the Atlantic Wall with bombs and shells. That was a good word to describe it, for the bombardment was to fall, literally, like rain.

The assault troops had every reason to hope that the Germans would be wiped out and their strongpoints shattered before the landings. As they listened to the thunder of the explosions, their confidence grew. The fantastic rumble of the battleships' gunfire was perhaps the most comforting noise of all. Their shells, amid the general booming rumble, sounded like freight cars rolling downgrade, high in the sky. They sounded as if they could blow up Normandy all by themselves.

So, despite their discomfort, the men in the boats felt keyed up. One section leader remembered afterward that his men jabbered away, as they came in, with great enthusiasm. They talked about what a mess the bombardment must be making of the Atlantic Wall.

"That place is going to be a shambles," one of them predicted.

Not until later, when the assault boats were within a few hundred yards of the shore, did the truth begin to come clear.

The fact was that an amazing number of Germans and German guns survived the heaviest bombardment in history.

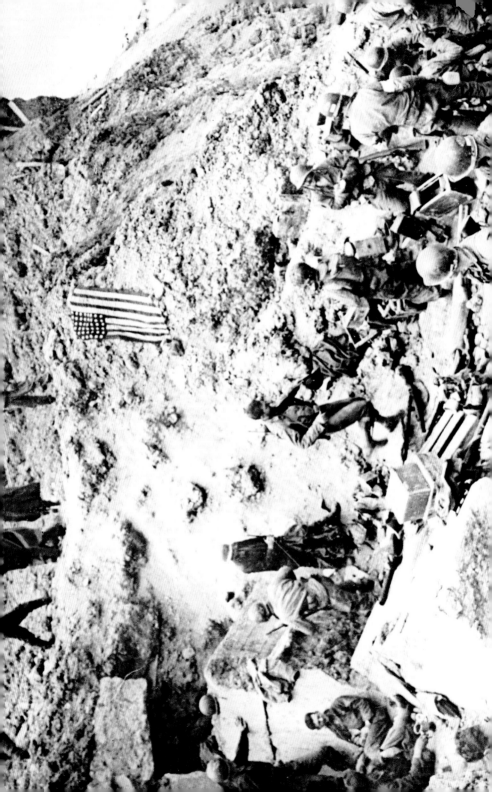

• CHAPTER THREE •

# OPERATION OVERLORD

World War II had started almost five years earlier, on September 1, 1939, when Germany invaded Poland. England and France had promised to defend Poland. But they were unprepared to fight, and as a result they were terribly beaten. By the next spring, France had fallen into German hands. The British army had to flee the Continent and escaped from the French port of Dunkirk with frightful losses. In the summer of 1940, the Nazi Germans, with their allies, the Italians, controlled all of western Europe. The German air force began its attempt to bomb the British Isles into rubble.

American troops shortly after landing in Normandy.

Nevertheless, the British immediately began to think about getting back onto the Continent. They started planning an attack across the Channel—even though it seemed more likely that they would become the invaded rather than the invaders.

Hitler threatened to invade England. He went so far as to assemble a fleet of barges along the French coast, planning to use them as assault boats. But he hesitated because he realized the risks of an amphibious attack. Also, he knew that the British Navy would destroy itself, if necessary, in an attempt to smash a German invasion fleet. Still, the idea was tempting.

The British knew as well as Hitler did that if the Germans could make the landing successfully, England would be lost. Some English homeowners, feeling that they would prefer death to surrender, got together pitchforks and filled pots with ordinary pepper to throw in the faces of the invading Germans. At one point, the British talked about stopping Hitler's assault by pouring oil and gasoline on the English Channel, setting fire to it, and burning the invasion barges— and the desperate idea at least made good propaganda.

Meanwhile, Royal Air Force fighter pilots, in their Spitfires and Hurricanes, lashed back at the great German air force, the *Luftwaffe*. And the British prime minister, Winston Churchill, and the British people looked forward to the day when England would attack.

Then Hitler postponed his English invasion plans. It was, from his point of view, one of his greatest errors. He made another bad mistake in June, 1941, by declaring war on

FOR FREEDOM

A BRITISH
"SPITFIRE"
ON PATROL

GERMAN PILOTS have learned to dread the British "Spitfire," which is so fast and so manœuvrable that it has accounted for hundreds of enemy bombers and fighters. "Spitfire" fighters escort bombers on their many daylight attacks on German-controlled industries on the Continent.

Russia, until then his ally. His Italian and Japanese partners also made mistakes. They both attempted more than they had the strength to handle. Italy pushed the war into North Africa. Japan brought the United States into the conflict, on December 7th of that same year, by attacking Hawaii (Pearl Harbor), the Philippines, and other American possessions in the Pacific.

American military strategists, like the British, began to plan for the day when the Allies would invade Europe to destroy the powerful German army.

In August, 1942, when the United States was just beginning to turn its peacetime strength into military power, the British and Canadians actually made a small, amphibious test raid across the Channel. It was aimed at the small French port of Dieppe. The raid was a disaster. Nearly half the 6,100 British and Canadian soldiers who took part in it were killed or captured.

Yet despite its frightful cost, the Dieppe raid taught the Allies a valuable lesson. This was that the built-up seaports, like Dieppe, were too well fortified to be attacked successfully, and that the great assault had better aim for open beaches.

But a large invasion, depending on great quantities of ammunition, gasoline, food, and countless other supplies, would need a port or excellent unloading facilities in France. So the raid inspired an idea which worked: The Allies would bring the port with them. On D-Day, they towed from England all the parts of two temporary ports which they put together off the flat Normandy beaches.

These included ships to be sunk as breakwaters and floating piers, cranes, and hoists.

Right after Dieppe, things began to go better for the Allies. In the fall of 1942, the British 8th Army, commanded by General Bernard Law Montgomery, defeated the Germans and Italians in Egypt—the first in a series of defeats that was to drive them out of the North African desert. And farther west, nearer the Atlantic side of Africa, a thousand-ship British and American invasion force landed. As it advanced to meet Montgomery, the enemy was caught in a powerful two-way squeeze.

In January, 1943, Prime Minister Churchill and President Franklin D. Roosevelt met at Casablanca in North Africa. By then they felt that the tide of the war had turned. The Russians had stopped the Germans at the Russian city of Stalingrad and were throwing them back from the Volga River. The North African campaign seemed certain to be a decisive success. While the next step was to knock Italy out of the war—no small matter—a joint staff of British and Americans started to plan in earnest for the great cross-Channel invasion.

They hoped it would be ready by early 1944. In May, 1943, they gave the project its code name. It was to be known as Operation Overlord.

# ⋆ SUPPORTING THE WAR ⋆

Because so many men were needed for the war effort, women were needed to take their places in the workforce. Posters and images like these encouraged women to seek employment. It was seen as a patriotic way to support the war, and was vital to keeping the country on its feet. After the war, the women were encouraged to return to being housewives or working in the traditionally "feminine" fields—some were happy to do so, and others were reluctant to give their new occupations back to the returning soldiers.

**Left:** Riveter at work on Consolidated bomber, Consolidated Aircraft Corp., Fort Worth, Texas.

**Below:** Woman working in an airplane factory.

- CHAPTER FOUR -

# MOUNTING THE ATTACK

The preparations for the great assault had been going on at full speed for two years. Their size and complexity were almost more than any man could grasp. Even at SHAEF (Supreme Headquarters, Allied Expeditionary Force), the brain center of the attack, only a few officers were in positions to appreciate everything that had been and was going on.

The men in the assault sections knew comparatively little about the big operation.

Just a small portion of the vast amount of equipment stockpiled in England prior to crossing the Channel for D-Day.

They realized, of course, that they were the spearhead of a mighty effort. But none of them knew that they were leading the way for a total force of more than 2.8 million men, including thirty-six divisions and the vast number of men, mostly in the supply services, that are required to keep a division on the battlefield. (A huge number, seemingly—unless you knew, as the officers at SHAEF knew, that the German commander, Field Marshal Gerd von Rundstedt, had about sixty divisions under his command in France.)

The assault troops understood, generally, the importance of what they were about to try to do. They had been impressed, nonetheless, by visits from both the army group commander, General Montgomery, and the man in command of the entire expeditionary force, General Dwight D. Eisenhower, who had talked briefly to nearly all the leading combat units.

But much of what had been going on was top secret. The men in the first boat sections observed the results of many actions they had heard practically nothing about.

○ ○ ○

They noticed, for instance, that there were no German planes in the sky.

But they didn't know why.

The answer involved a fabulous battle story—of air battle, in this case—that had been fought and won as one part of the D-Day preparations.

At this critical moment, the Germans had fewer than 200 fighter planes available for the defense of France. Most of those they had were not going to get off the ground—for lack of gasoline. Most of those that took to the air were not going to fight—primarily because they were so heavily outnumbered.

That was a sign of one great job the Allied air forces had done. For two years our bombers had been destroying Germany's gasoline-refining and plane-manufacturing factories. This was just as important as meeting and defeating German planes in the air. In the two months before the assault, the Allied airmen had set out to wreck the railroads the German army would need for a counterattack. In April and May, 1,437 French locomotives had been bombed or machine-gunned out of action. And the secret Allied helpers in France—the men and women in the French resistance movement—had blown up another 292.

We had already won the war in the air at the cost of thousands of American and British lives. Without that earlier victory, the assault would have been foolhardy.

But the men in the assault boats knew very little about the air war. They had not been briefed on the fact that the German fighter-plane force had been crippled beyond recovery in air battles in February, 1944. So decisive was this victory that the commander of the American air forces, General H. H. Arnold, compared it to the Battle of Gettysburg for its importance in American history.

The leading ground troops merely noted the results. They were glad to see that all the planes in the sky were striped with painted bands like Christmas candy—meaning that they belonged to the Allies, not to the Germans.

◉ ◉ ◉

# THE FRENCH RESISTANCE

While the French are sometimes wrongly criticized for their lack of defense against the Germans in World War II, in reality, the brave fighters of the French Resistance provided key assistance to the Allied invasion of June, 1944.

The French Resistance, a loosely formed organization of civilian guerilla fighters and conspirators, provided key intelligence on the German military installations making up the Atlantic Wall, and they carried out critical acts of sabotage on electrical power installations, transportation networks, and telephone and telegraph lines. They also established a network of escape safe houses that helped rescue airmen shot down over France and transport them back to Allied territory.

At the time of the Normandy invasion, the French resistance movement included fully 100,000 people, and grew rapidly as the German strength in France lessened.

An American officer and a French resistance fighter are seen engaged in a street battle with German forces in the photo above.

It was obvious, in the same way, that the German navy hadn't been able to interfere with the Channel crossing. There had been no signs of German submarines or torpedo boats. The Allied navies had won complete control of the invasion's sea routes.

The men in the landing boats were delighted that the approach sail had gone so smoothly, but they did not understand how it had happened.

The answer was that our command of the sea was the result of months of round-the-clock fighting over the whole Atlantic Ocean, from the Arctic Circle to the Cape of Good Hope.

One of the Allied navies' greatest successes had been won only the day before D-Day. Late on the afternoon of June 5th, British, Canadian, and American mine sweepers had finished clearing ten separate paths through the fields of floating mines that the Germans had sown in the English Channel. It had been an even more dangerous job for the small boats than mine sweeping usually is because the Channel's tidal currents are unusually strong. But the small boats had done it. They had made the Allied invasion fleet's crossing safe.

Since the assault troops hadn't known much about the danger of mines, they could hardly appreciate what the mine sweepers had done. The soldiers were more interested, having been the sailors' guests for several days, in arguing whether navy food was better than army food. Most of them thought it was. The American soldiers were especially envious of the navy's white bread because they had been eating (and not liking) English bread that was slightly brown in color.

The sheer weight of the invasion force was almost beyond calculation.

The British Isles are not much bigger than the state of Colorado. On the eve of the assault, they were so jampacked with men and assault equipment that it was almost funny—if it hadn't been so deadly serious.

It seemed as if all the open fields along all the English country roads had been turned into parking lots. The Americans alone needed parking space for 50,000 jeeps and trucks, and 44,000,000 square feet of out-of-doors storage space.

We had shipped in 20,000 railroad cars and 1,000 steam engines just to move our own men and supplies around England.

Within the first two weeks after D-Day, the Allies hoped to put ashore 725,000 men and 95,000 vehicles. The preparation involved in moving such an enormous force, and all the supplies required, was among the most complicated and difficult problems any military staff has ever had to face.

It took more than 6,000 vessels to accomplish the task, including landing craft, merchant transports, and naval fighting ships.

The Allies had had to plan to load, move, and then unload more than 200,000 tons of supplies within those first fourteen days. Once the invasion force was completely ashore in France, it was expected to burn at least a million gallons of gasoline a day.

Small wonder that southern England had been transformed into what looked like a great open-air warehouse!

◦   ◦   ◦

The planning had involved more than stockpiling and moving mountains of matériel. Operation Overlord had taken a fantastic amount of detailed study and calculation.

There had been experts of a hundred kinds working on the countless items of information, technique, and equipment that were about to be tested. Among these items, to mention just a few, were long-range weather predictions, waterproofing methods, seasickness pills, radio communications networks, concentrated foods, uniforms, camouflage, and new weapons. The experts had worked unceasingly, aware that they would never know all the answers to many questions they had been asked to solve.

Maps—to take just one detail—were a good example.

From the moment the landing beaches had been chosen, which was in May, 1943, intelligence officers studied photographs of the ground as if they were looking for pennies in the sand. They tried to learn every possible fact about the fifty-mile strip: Just where was the high-water mark? How big were the grains of sand? Would the stony shingle just beyond the sand support a two-and-a-half-ton truck? Where were the best exits from the beaches? Did these show as roads, or cart tracks, or dry stream lines? And, above all, exactly what had the Germans done to fortify them?

Men had risked their lives in low-flying planes and in sneak raids to get information. General Omar N. Bradley,

Some of the first assault troops to hit the Normandy beachhead take cover behind enemy obstacles to fire on German forces as others follow the first tanks plunging through the water towards the German-held shore.

who commanded the American ground troops, tells of one British lieutenant who had been taken in a submarine one night through the minefields in the Channel. Then he had paddled ashore, under the muzzles of the German guns, in a tiny rubber boat. All he wanted was a sample of sand from a certain spot. He got it. And as a result, the planners knew that the ground at that place was sandy and firm, not muddy as they had feared it might be.

All the information was evaluated and then compiled on maps. There were even foam-rubber scale models of the beaches which rolled up like rugs for storage in tubular map cases. Just before sailing time, each assault section was given such a model of its own part of the beach to learn by heart.

There had never been better war maps.

○   ○   ○

Special training had been another big job.

The men in the assault boats knew a lot about that. They had been rehearsing their work for months.

They were in the best possible physical condition. Every one of them could do twenty-five push-ups, run three hundred yards in forty-five seconds or less, crawl fifty yards under barbed wire, carry a man piggy-back for twenty-five yards, and then, without stopping to catch their breaths, march four miles in forty-five minutes.

Every man could swim at least fifty yards wearing his uniform, his boots, and his helmet. (Those who hadn't been able to swim before had learned. They had been swimming through the cold English winter in rivers, streams, and emergency water tanks which were part of England's air-raid defense equipment.)

They had all taken part in at least three large-scale dress rehearsals for the assault. They had come in by boat to English beaches which were almost exactly like the real targets in France. Every man had had a chance to do his job in practices so much like the real thing that the troops couldn't tell they were make-believe—until they saw that instead of Germans shooting back they were met by umpires waving brightly colored flags.

(At one of the rehearsals, in April, German S-boats had attacked the mock invasion fleet. They sank two large landing ships; more than 700 Allied men had been lost.)

Of course a battle can only be rehearsed up to a certain point. Still, the sham battles had gone about as far as possible toward being the real thing.

# CHAPTER FIVE

# IKE SAYS "GO!"

In spite of all the rehearsals, no one had been sure, until just before it happened, when the invasion would actually take place.

By Saturday, June 3rd, the troops were all loaded on board the transports and ready to go. But at the last minute it looked as if the attack might have to be postponed for two weeks or a month. The trouble was with the weather, which is beyond the control of any plan.

US Coast Guard LCI, heavily listing to port, moves alongside a transport ship to evacuate her troops, during the initial Normandy landing operations in France, on June 6, 1944. Moments later the craft will capsize and sink. Note that helmeted infantrymen, with full packs, are all standing to starboard side of the ship.

Only a few days in the whole year were right for the assault.

It couldn't have been before June, because the last of the landing craft hadn't been delivered.

There had to be a full moon at night so the paratroopers could see.

A rising tide, from a low before dawn to a high around the middle of the morning, was needed to clear anti-landing obstacles in the water and to land the assault boats.

In June, only the 5th, 6th, and 7th days had both the right phase of the moon and the right tides at the right hours.

But on Saturday, the 3rd, the weather was bad and the forecast was discouraging. By Sunday it was clear that Monday, the 5th, would be hopeless. The prediction was for weather so bad that the air forces wouldn't be able to deliver their all-important bombardment. General Eisenhower postponed the attack for twenty-four hours.

The question was whether it could be made on the 6th.

It was one of the hardest decisions a man has ever had to make. Bad weather could ruin the assault. But so could another postponement. To delay any longer meant that the enemy might break the secrecy with which the plans were guarded. The huge invasion force, all brought together in southern England, was a big, easy target for Nazi bombers, or for the new pilotless aircraft which, the Allies knew, Hitler was just about to unveil. And what would postponement do to the men's morale? That was perhaps the greatest of the dangers in waiting. The assault troops were at a high pitch of readiness. It would be hard, if not impossible, to reach it a second time.

On Sunday night, June 4th, General Eisenhower met with his main advisers in a large room in a mansion called Southwick House. It was near the town of Portsmouth on the south coast of England and it was used as headquarters for Admiral Sir Bertram H. Ramsay, who commanded the naval forces. The wind was blowing furiously, and the rain came down in torrents.

The invasion's nine top commanders sat in an informal group in library chairs, surrounded by bookshelves that were mostly empty, and listened to the final reports by three weather experts.

Group Captain J.M. Stagg, SHAEF's chief meteorologist, said that all three agreed that the weather was going to get better. The winds were going to die down a good deal. The rain would stop. It was going to be very cloudy over Normandy on Tuesday morning, but they thought it would be clear enough for the bombers to see the German strongpoints that were their targets.

General Eisenhower took a poll of his advisers. Both Air Chief Marshal Sir Arthur W. Tedder, who was the deputy supreme commander, second only to Eisenhower, and Air Chief Marshal Sir Trafford Leigh-Mallory, the air commander, were doubtful. They thought the air forces would not be able to do their job in heavily overcast skies. "Chancy" was the word they used.

Fully equipped, and each carrying large amounts of ammunition, American troops climb aboard a landing craft somewhere in England on June 6, 1944, for the cross-channel invasion of France.

Eisenhower turned to Montgomery, the commander of all the ground forces.

"Do you see any reason for not going Tuesday?" Eisenhower asked.

There had not been many times when Montgomery hadn't been eager to fight.

"I would say—go!" Montgomery answered.

Eisenhower listened to everybody. Near the end of the conversation he pointed out that not going was chancy, too. He thought the question was just how long the invasion could be left "hanging on the end of a limb."

A supreme commander can ask for advice, as Eisenhower had done, but there is no way in the world that he can get anybody to make his decisions for him. Everybody in the room knew that. General Walter Bedell Smith, Eisenhower's chief of staff, was struck by the terrible loneliness of his commander at that moment. Eisenhower was surrounded by his most trusted colleagues, and yet no one could really help him. He had to make the fateful choice all by himself.

He thought it over.

"I don't see how we can do anything else," he said.

The word was—"Go!"

· CHAPTER SIX ·

# OUT OF THE SKY

The paratroopers went first. There were two separate drops fifty miles apart, one on each end of the invasion area, and both of them inland, behind the Germans' beach defenses. The paratroopers began dropping out of the night sky at 1:30 a.m., five hours before the seaborne attack started. They were preceding the main assault. No one had a tougher job.

The larger of the two drops was on the west, on the Cotentin Peninsula, behind Utah beach. It involved two American airborne divisions, the 101st and the 82nd: a total of 12,000 parachutists jumping out of 925 troop carrier planes and then,

US paratroopers fix their static lines before a jump before dawn over Normandy on D-Day.

somewhat later, 4,000 men in 500 gliders. These troops were to set the stage for the attack on Utah beach.

They were to seize key roads and bridges far behind Utah, and to throw the Germans guarding the area into confusion. One of their most important aims was to control several built-up causeways that led from the beach across a large swamp just behind it. Those causeways, like all the exits from the beaches along the entire front, had to be taken. They were the routes that the invasion, once ashore, would have to follow on its way inland.

British paratroopers of the 6th Airborne Division were dropped on the east end of the invasion front, behind Sword beach. They were supposed to hold the bridges across the Orne River and the Caen Canal, which the Allies hoped to use. They were also to blow up the bridges over the Dives River, farther east, so the Germans could not bring reinforcements across them. They were also ordered to capture a large German gun battery at a town called Merville. In all, the paratroopers were supposed to take an area of twenty-four square miles.

The moon was full, as expected. But on the American side, thick clusters of low-hanging clouds blanketed the ground. The carrier planes, flying in tight V-formations, glided down toward jump level, 600 feet above the ground. The paratroopers stood up, ready to dive out into the black unknown below. But then, in many cases, the planes flew into the cloud layer. It was like sliding into a pea-soup fog. The planes had to veer apart, spreading open their close formations, in order to avoid colliding with each other. It meant that when the paratroopers hit the ground they were scattered all over the landscape.

That was bad.

A night drop of this size was an experiment. A lot depended, everyone knew, on the paratroopers' first minutes on the ground. They had to get rid of their chutes, find the bundles of equipment that had been dropped for them, and then find one another fast. For until they had assembled into sizable fighting units, the Germans could pick them off by ones, twos, or threes.

The clouds covered the moon and darkness, in itself, made assembly hard. And then the scattering was so bad that some units were to spend all of D-Day just trying to find one another and get organized. Men in the 101st Division came down as far away as twenty miles from where they were supposed to be. More than half of the division's bundles of weapons and ammunition was lost because it fell into swamps or into fields that the Germans controlled. And the 82nd Division's drop, on the whole, was more badly scattered than the 101st's.

As a result, instead of one large battle, the paratroopers found themselves fighting fifteen or twenty small separate actions.

And instead of fighting in their regular units, many of the soldiers fought in groups that had put themselves together on the ground. The men in them had never seen one another before.

Nobody knew what was happening. Radio communications, in the mixup, broke down. Several times, groups of paratroopers fought only a few hundred yards away from each other without the faintest idea that they had friends close at hand. And scarcely more than a third of the men managed to join and fight with any one of the dozens of small groups that did assemble.

Casualties were heavy. Every fifth man was wounded, killed, or taken prisoner before the end of D-Day.

After the Normandy invasion, we never again dropped parachute troops at night.

And yet, in spite of all that went wrong, the air drop behind Utah beach was a success. For although the paratroopers were confused, they confused the Germans even more.

At 1:30, German Corps headquarters reported to German Army headquarters that the paratroopers were landing. But, on account of the scattering, the Germans couldn't tell how big the attack was. By 2:30, they had diagnosed the situation fairly accurately. However, Field Marshal von Rundstedt, at his Army Group headquarters in a villa near Paris, decided that the paratroopers were not part of a major Allied attack. All through the night, the German high command failed to take the airborne assault seriously enough.

The Germans on the actual ground were just as hesitant as those at headquarters.

They fought hard when the paratroopers attacked, but they were slow to move. They couldn't make any sense out of the pattern of the drops—and no wonder! So, instead of leaping to the offensive and going out to hunt the Americans while they were at their weakest, most of the Germans sat tight in their prepared defensive positions.

That was all the paratroopers needed. Sections of the 101st, picking up men as they moved forward, struck sharply toward the inland ends of the causeways from Utah beach. By 4:30, part of a battalion of the 82nd had rushed into the village of Ste. Mère Eglise, and had raised an American flag over it. (It was the same flag the same unit had raised when they entered Naples.)

Ste. Mère Eglise was important from a military standpoint, since several roads met and crossed there. The battalion used only their knives, bayonets, and hand grenades in their bold attack. By so doing they knew, whenever they heard a gun fire and saw its muzzle flash, that the Germans were doing the shooting. The battalion cut the main German communications cable to Cherbourg, and set up several roadblocks outside Ste. Mère Eglise. And, although the Germans fought for the village until well into the night of D-Day, the paratroopers held on.

The smaller British drop behind the eastern end of the beaches went more easily. There was less trouble with clouds and fog and the paratroopers were not so badly scattered. The British sent in six gliders right at the start of their drop. Four of them slid down out of the sky with marvelous accuracy and landed as they were supposed to, right on the bridges across the Orne River and the Caen Canal. (The British code names for these bridges were "Cricket" and "Rugger," the two most popular English sports.) Paratroopers, with their faces blackened so they wouldn't show up as spots of white in the dark, dashed out of the big motorless ships. The bridges were theirs in minutes, before the Germans quite woke up to the fact that a parachute and glider assault was going on.

The attack on the Dives River bridges went just as well.

# ★ THE GLIDER INFANTRY ★

Although the paratroopers were more highly regarded and got more of the glory, the infantry members who landed behind enemy lines in gliders in many ways had the more dangerous duties.

Each glider was made of plywood and held between thirteen and twenty-five soldiers, plus a quantity of equipment. Towed into airspace near the drop zone by powered aircraft, such as a C-47, the pilot of the gliders came down into the French countryside at very steep angles in pitch darkness, hoping to find a relatively smooth landing spot free of the booby-trap spikes (nicknamed "Rommel's aspara-

gus") planted by the Germans around the countryside.

In most cases, the brittle plywood aircraft broke apart on landing at eighty miles per hour, and while some lost their crews entirely, other gliders landed somewhat intact, and their well-trained crews quickly regrouped. Unlike the parachutists, who were badly scattered as they landed and sometimes required several days to regroup into fighting units, the glider infantry landed more or less intact as a unit, complete with weapons and equipment, and could move forward with their assignments fairly quickly. Because they landed silently

(except for the sometimes-notable sound of crashing), the glider infantry often avoided enemy attention and could sometimes surprise the relaxed troops guarding bridges and other targets. Some glider infantry units succeeded quickly in their missions to capture key bridges.

**Above left:** Gliders of an American airborne division, their mission completed, lie wrecked in a field in France, on June 10, 1944. **Above:** Airborne Troops on their way to a Horsa Glider at a Heavy Glider Conversion Unit, somewhere in the Home Counties, England, on October 9, 1943. **Inset:** British Horsa gliders and parachutes after Allied Airborne landings in a field north east of Caen, France, on June 10, 1944. The fuselage of the gliders are not broken as it would appear, but are detachable from the wings, enabling the glider to be unloaded quickly.

At the same time, another group set out to capture the big German gun battery at Merville, whose guns could wreck the assault boat formations if they were firing at H-Hour. When the heavy RAF bombers came over at 3:15, they tried to knock out the battery. They missed it, but the bombardment nearly killed the paratroopers. After the bombers left, the paratroopers got up and took the battery the hard way, attacking through barbed wire and over minefields. And Hitler's Atlantic Wall was thereby minus one of its strongpoints.

⊚ ⊚ ⊚

## D-DAY, A GERMAN PRIVATE'S VIEW: JUNE 6, 1944

*On that night of 6 June none of us expected the invasion any more. There was a strong wind, thick cloud cover, and the enemy aircraft had not bothered us more that day than usual. But then—in the night—the air was full of innumerable planes. We thought, "What are they demolishing tonight?" But then it started. I was at the wireless set myself. One message followed the other. "Parachutists landing here—gliders landing there," and finally "Landing craft approaching." Some of our guns fired as best they could. In the morning a huge naval force was sighted—that was the last report our advanced observation posts could send us, before they were overwhelmed. And it was the last report we received about the situation. It was no longer possible to get an idea of what was happening. Wireless communications were jammed, the cables cut, and our* officers had lost grasp of the situation. Infantrymen who were streaming back told us that their new positions on the coast had been overrun or that the few "bunkers" in our sector had either been shot up or blown to pieces.

Right in the middle of all this turmoil, I got orders to go with my car for a reconnaissance towards the coast. With a few infantrymen, I reported to a lieutenant. His orders were to retake a village nearby. While he was still talking to me to explain the position, a British tank came rolling towards us from behind, from a direction in which we had not even suspected the presence of the enemy. The enemy tank immediately opened fire on us. Resistance was out of the question. I saw how a group of Polish infantrymen went over to the enemy—carrying their submachine-guns and waving their arms. When we tried to get through to our lines in the evening, British paratroopers caught us.

At first I was rather depressed, of course. I, an old soldier, was a prisoner of war after a few hours of the invasion. But when I saw the material behind the enemy front, I could only say, "Old man, how lucky you have been!"

And when the sun rose the next morning, I saw the invasion fleet lying off the shore. Ship beside ship. And without a break, troops, weapons, tanks, munitions, and vehicles were being unloaded in a steady stream.

# ★ WOMEN IN THE MILITARY ★

Many women were eager to serve in the military in whatever capacity they could, and the military, stretched thin, eventually took them in for non-combat roles. The Women's Airforce Service Pilots (WASP), the Women's Army Corps (WAC), and the United States Naval Reserve (Women's Reserve—better known as the Women Accepted for Volunteer Emergency Service: WAVES), the United States Coast Guard Women's Reserve (known as SPARS), and the United States Marine Corps Women's Reserve were all created during World War II.

The 1,704 WASP pilots flew over 60 million miles, crisscrossing the country. There were

over 80,000 WAVES serving in 900 bases across the US during the war, and about 150,000 women served in the WAC during this time. Like their Navy counterparts, most WAC women served in the US, but some were sent across the world—including those who landed at Normandy a few weeks after the D-Day invasion. Eisenhower said of the WACs that "their contributions in efficiency, skill, spirit, and determination are immeasurable."

Twenty thousand women served in the Marine Corps Women's Reserve during the war; it was the last branch of the military to accept women, and did not have a nickname like the others. The approximately 11,000 SPARS served in every USCG district except Puerto Rico.

The WASP was disbanded shortly following the war and its pilots had to fight to attain official veterans' status. The other four divisions, under the Women's Armed Services Integration Act of 1948, merged into the permanent armed forces divisions—though it was some time before they were allowed the same roles as men.

# CHAPTER SEVEN

# BAD WEATHER

The parachute and glider landings had thrown the Germans off balance. That in itself was worth as much as any of the specific objectives the paratroopers took. Hours after the airborne assault had actually started, the German generals were still clinging to the idea that it was part of a hoax.

They thought that the real invasion would come in farther north, at the Pas de Calais, the French side of the narrowest part of the English Channel.

They thought, in short, that the paratroopers' lead-off jab was only a feint.

This is the scene along a section of Omaha Beach. Seen in the background is part of the large fleet that brought the Allied troops across the English Channel. Barrage balloons are flying in the air, designed to entangle low-flying enemy aircraft in their cables.

General Erwin Rommel, who shared the German anti-invasion command with General von Rundstedt, had said: "We must stop the assaulting forces in the water, not only delaying, but destroying all enemy equipment while still afloat."

The time had come for the Germans to try.

But Rommel, as able and energetic a commander as Hitler had, was not on duty. He was in Stuttgart, Germany, celebrating his wife's birthday. He had stopped to see her, briefly, on his way back to his headquarters from a command visit with Hitler.

The Germans in France hesitated, for the moment, to make their move.

The bad weather, which had caused the Allied commanders so much worry, had a lot to do with the Germans' failure to understand what was happening. The weather had been so bad that they had canceled their regular air and sea reconnaissance patrols. It had improved only a little. The Germans were sure that the Allies wouldn't dare risk the main invasion effort until the seas had calmed and the skies had cleared.

And indeed, just before H-Hour it began to look as if the Allies' gamble on the weather might have been too bold.

The paratroopers were managing in spite of the clouds, but the overcast at six o'clock was too heavy for the bombardiers of the United States Eighth Air Force. They couldn't see their targets, the German strongpoints on the beaches. They had to bomb by instrument, which was far less accurate. Moreover, in order to make sure that they would not hit any of our own assault boats now closing in on the beaches, the bombardiers had been ordered to wait as much as thirty seconds after they came over the coast before releasing their bombs. As a result of all this, the bombardiers missed their targets. Instead of smashing the German beach defenses, they dropped their 3,000 tons of bombs into the green Normandy fields. In most cases the earth-shaking blasts did little more than tear open craters in cow pastures, horrifying hundreds of cows.

The weather had taken the sting out of one vital part of the assault plan.

And the weather was winning another victory over an important Allied weapon. The waves were too high for the amphibious tanks, called DD (for dual-drive) tanks. They were a secret and most clever invention—34-ton Sherman tanks that could "swim." They had collapsible canvas-and-rubber sides filled with air to make the tanks float and to keep the water out of their turret hatches, large ventilators sticking up high in back to get rid of the engines' exhaust fumes and to supply the carburetors with air, and small propellers to drive them through the water. The DD tanks were to "swim" ashore with the first of the infantry assault boats. Their guns were expected to be a tremendous help between the time the air-sea bombardment ended and the arrival of the artillery that was due to follow the infantry assault sections ashore.

A DD tank rode very low in the water. All of the tank itself was underwater, with just a foot or two of the siding, the gun, and the turret showing. That meant that even in

RAF planes, towing gliders, are silhouetted in the light of dawn on D-Day over the English channel.

slightly choppy seas, there was great danger that waves could spill into their open tops and sink the tanks.

Although the wind had died down, as H-Hour approached it was still blowing from the northwest at more than ten miles an hour. The breakers off the beach, in most places, were three or four feet high. Omaha, the more important of the two American beaches, was feeling the worst of what was left of the storm.

General Omar N. Bradley, who, under Montgomery's overall command of the ground forces, was in charge of the American section of the seaborne troops, was on the open bridge of the cruiser *Augusta* a few thousand yards off Omaha. His staff operations officer, Colonel Truman C. Thorson, was beside him. He was nicknamed "Tubby" because he was remarkably thin.

Bradley recalls in his book, *A Soldier's Story*, that both of them were squinting through binoculars, trying to see what was happening. The shore itself was hidden by the fog, but they could easily see that the waters between the *Augusta* and Omaha beach, now swarming with assault craft, were dangerously rough. Thorson said he thought the DDs were going to have a hard time getting through the sea.

"Yes, Tubby, I'm afraid you're right," Bradley said. "But at this point there's nothing we can do."

"Any sign of a letup in the surf?"

"Not yet," Bradley said.

The tanks that tried to swim ashore were in as much trouble as Bradley feared. They began to suffer damage from the moment they were launched. Waves smashed the canvas-and-rubber siding. Water flooded their engine compartments. One battalion of thirty-two tanks, headed for the eastern half of Omaha, lost twenty-seven on the way in. They sank while their crews struggled to keep afloat in life preservers and hoped that rescue boats would see them and pick them up. (Most of the men were saved.) Of the five DDs from that battalion that got ashore, only two swam in under their own power. The other three were taken all the way in to the beach by the LCT (Landing Craft, Tank) that had brought them across the Channel. That was done because the LCT's bow ramp, which was supposed to open at sea, wouldn't work. So, since it couldn't launch them according to plan, the LCT delivered its tanks to the shore.

It was the same story along the whole coast. Half the tanks due on Sword, the easternmost British beach, sank. Most of those that got ashore were put ashore. That's how they were landed on Gold, the British beach nearest Omaha. But it was far too late for the generals and admirals to order all the LCTs to beach themselves along with their DD tanks. The tank detachment commanders had to decide what to do by themselves. Many were slow to change the plan because it took longer to bring the tanks in than to let them swim in, and the commanders were afraid the DDs would touch down too late to help the infantry when it would need help the most. And they were right. All the way from Utah to Sword—with some exceptions—DD tanks were either missing or late.

H-Hour was at hand.

Among the first to land on the Normandy beaches were Royal Navy Commandoes whose task was to remove various types of obstructions embedded by the enemy in the sands. High explosives and mines were attached to many of these obstructions.

The assault sections were ending their long run in. It was just as well that they—especially the men about to touch down on Omaha—didn't realize that the weather had crippled both their air and tank support.

# CHAPTER EIGHT

# FIRST WAVES

The crucial moment had come.

The next three or four hours would answer the awesome question. The assault sections would or would not break through the Atlantic Wall. The invaders would or would not win the first small toehold on the French coast.

The enormous weight of the whole gigantic effort rested entirely, for the time being, on the men in the first waves.

Everything depended on them. And, during the decisive first hours, there was nothing anyone else could do to help. What could be done had already

American invasion troops stop for a breather under a protecting chalk cliff after wading ashore on the French coast on June 9, 1944.

been done. Those things that had already failed were beyond correction.

All that counted, now, were the LCVPs and the thirty-two-man teams aboard them.

It made no difference, at H-Hour, how many millions of men were waiting, ready to follow. Or how many tons of supplies had been assembled. Or how many people, all over the world, were counting on the invasion to succeed.

What mattered now was whether a substantial number of these few thousand men could manage to unload from the small boats, wade ashore, cross the beaches, and fight their way inland for at least a few hundred yards.

*   *   *

It was a moment of nearly unbearable drama. Modern warfare, we think, is a matter of science, invention, factory production, and all the other measures of nations' power. As indeed, in the large sense, it is.

But at H-Hour on D-Day, the situation in the large sense suddenly faded in importance.

The spotlight turned on the individual men in action.

Each member of each first-wave assault section had countless assistants backing him up. These were not only the service men in the assault, the reinforcements in England, the troops on their way overseas, and those in training in all the Allied countries, but also millions of civilians who were engaged in war work and war production. So each man in the first-wave assault section represented everything that those "behind him"—as the phrase went—had accomplished.

For all of that, the first-wave troops were men with names and home addresses.

What they needed most, at the moment, was courage.

And courage was something that couldn't be issued like helmets or hand grenades.

It was, in fact, a most mysterious quality. No one knew, at H-Hour, just who had it, or how much of it. Veterans of other landings, some of whom had performed with amazing courage in the past, weren't sure how much of it they had left. The green soldiers, including those who were about to act with extraordinary gallantry, were nearly all afraid that they might not have enough of it. And some of the first-wave troops, feeling themselves in the grip of unmanageable fear, already felt, secretly, that they were not going to be able to carry out their specific assignments.

⊚　⊚　⊚

Whatever the answer was about to be, it was an individual, man-by-man answer.

If the first holes in the Atlantic Wall were going to be opened, mere men would do the job.

And, while the assault was by boat section, each thirty-two-man group would remember—whether anyone else knew about it or not—who had contributed the most at each critical moment.

In that sense, the modern battle was precisely like every ancient battle; it depended on the bravery of the few who led the way.

⊚　⊚　⊚

A Canadian soldier removing a detonator from one of many mines the Germans left behind when they retreated.

No one was more aware of this than the assault commanders. Their men had been well trained. Now there was nothing more the commanders could do to influence the outcome. They had to wait to see whether the first waves, in addition to everything else they needed, had courage in sufficient supply.

"Overlord had run beyond the reach of its admirals and generals," General Bradley wrote later, describing the hours of agonizing suspense. "For the next few tortured hours we could do little but pace our decks and trust in the men to whom The Plan had been given for execution."

# CHAPTER NINE

# THE GERMAN DEFENDERS

The Germans began to shoot back. They had been deceptively quiet, stunned by the preparatory bombardment. But the moment the naval gunfire stopped, it became clear that the Atlantic Wall, for all the punishment it had taken, had by no means been shattered.

On Utah, where the 82nd and 101st airborne divisions were already taking up most of the German defenders' attention, resistance was comparatively light. The coastal guns fired a few artillery shells, set to burst in the air and shower the assault boats with fragments. But at the actual

Marshal Karl Gerd von Rundstedt, supreme commander of German forces in Western Europe on June 13, 1944, leads fellow military leaders in an inspection of the Atlantic Wall prior to D-Day.

moment of the touchdown on the beach, when twenty assault sections of the 4th Infantry Division waded out of the surf, the Germans were silent.

It was a quite different story on Omaha and on the three beaches to the east, Gold, Juno, and Sword. There the coastal defenses came to life suddenly and started firing with weapons of all sizes. German artillery shells, fired from near the town of Vierville on the western edge of Omaha, hit and sank an LCT loaded with tanks. Another shell scored a direct hit on a small assault boat that belonged to the Army-Navy Special Engineer Task Force. This had the hard job of blasting paths through the anti-landing obstacles before the tide, coming in fast, covered them with water. The engineers' boat was packed with TNT and coils of primacord fuse. When the shell burst, it set off the explosives. All the men on board were killed.

Five assault sections of Company A of the 29th Division's 116th Infantry Regiment came in at almost the same place—in front of the Vierville draw. Their boats grounded in water about five feet deep when they were still some distance from shore. Just as the boats stuck, the Germans opened up on them with intense artillery, machine-gun, and mortar fire. The boats' ramps went down. The soldiers started ashore in three files: first the center file and then the flank files who were supposed to peel off to the right and left to keep the men from bunching and making too good a target. But some were hit immediately, and all attempts to keep any kind of formation were given up. Some men tried to dive under water to get out of sight. Others kept moving forward, but the Germans raked the surf with bullets. Men were killed or wounded almost every step of the way. Those who got as far as the edge of the breakers saw that the gunfire on the beach was even worse, and many thought, in their desperation, that the water offered protection. A good many lay in the shallows just off the shore, in panic or exhaustion. Those near the anti-landing obstacles tried to take cover behind them. But the water was no real protection. It was only a matter of time before something hit the men who tried to take cover in it. Then those who were wounded were drowned because they couldn't keep ahead of the fast-moving, rising tide.

In a matter of minutes, every one of Company A's officers and most of its sergeants had been killed or wounded. Its total casualties were about two out of every three men. In fifteen minutes, the company was out of action.

German fire was just as hot on the eastern end of Omaha where the 1st Division's 16th Infantry Regiment came ashore. Crossing bands of machine-gun fire caught the assault boats as their ramps went down. Company E lost 105 of its 192 men. Most of them were hit while they waded ashore or when they stopped at the water's edge to drag wounded comrades onto the sand and out of the reach of the rising tide. Two sections of Company F landed in front of the Colleville draw. Colleville was a small town with a German strongpoint in it, like Vierville, and its strongpoint was very much in action. Twenty of the men in the two boats were casualties before they got to the shingle (the rocky, slightly raised part of the beach beyond the flat sands). Three of the other Company F sections waded into a hail of German fire. Only seven of the thirty-two men in one boat got across the beach. Only two of all the company's officers survived the first few minutes of the assault.

Gold beach, ten miles east of Omaha, was hardly any better. That was the sector assigned to the British 50th Division. Both the 1st Hampshires, landing near the town of Le Hamel, and the 5th East Yorkshires, near La Rivière, ran into heavy artillery fire. Machine-gun bullets sprayed across the beaches. Both the bombings and the naval shelling had missed a great many of the German positions. During the preliminary bombardment of Gold, one of the German strongpoints had started a gun duel with HMS *Bulolo,* part of the British navy's bombardment squadron. HMS *Ajax,* another warship, came in and silenced the battery. But that was only one battery.

On Juno, where the 3rd Canadian Division came ashore, four tough German strongpoints were blazing away. In addition to mortars and machine guns, there were 50-millimeter, 75-millimeter, and 88-millimeter guns, aimed to sweep the sands from either end. Behind them were heavier artillery set to shoot at the landing craft. Eighty percent of the fortifications on Juno were still in working condition at H-Hour.

Sword, the easternmost of all the beaches, was as bad as Juno. It was the target of the British 3rd Division, which Montgomery had commanded in France in 1940, and which was now in action for the first time since Dunkirk. The 3rd had to hurry to take the three main strongpoints on Sword and push through to relieve the airborne men of the 6th Division behind the German lines. One assault boat commander, Major C. K. King of the East Yorkshires, had been reading to his men passages from Shakespeare's play *Henry V,* which tells of the English invasion of France in 1415:

> *On, on you noblest English,*
> *Whose blood is fet from fathers of war-proof!*
> *Fathers that, like so many Alexanders,*
> *Have in these parts from morn till even fought,*
> *And sheath'd their swords for lack of argument.*
> *Dishonour not your mothers; now attest*
> *That those whom you call'd fathers did beget you.*
> *Be copy now to men of grosser blood,*
> *And teach them how to war. . . .*

The major's literary effort was in the East Yorkshires' best tradition. One hundred and eighty-five years earlier, in the French and Indian War, the regiment had taken part in the capture of Quebec. On that occasion, the British army's commander, General James Wolfe, had read Gray's "Elegy" as he approached the city.

Not only was the German gunfire savage, but the tidal currents off Sword were especially strong. The 3rd Division needed all the inspiration, poetic or otherwise, it could get.

## ★ WAR CORRESPONDENTS ★

World War II was the first war in which American journalists regularly traveled with the troops, sharing the discomforts and dangers of life in a war zone. Some 1,600 reporters were accredited by the US military as war correspondents, including 127 women. Among the ranks of American war correspondents were journalist Ernie Pyle, "the GI's best friend," who was killed by a Japanese machine gunner during the Okinawa campaign in 1945, and photographer Margaret Bourke-White, who was in Moscow when the Germans invaded Russia, survived the torpedoing of the transport ship Strathallan by a U-boat in the Mediterranean, and was the first American woman ever to fly on an air combat mission. In the photo above, Associated Press staffer Marion Coleman, wearing combat gear, covers a US Army training exercise in 1943. At right, another Associated Press reporter, Henry Jameson, aboard the battleship USS *Arkansas* after sustaining an injury on D-Day.

# CHAPTER TEN

# THE RANGERS AT POINTE DU HOC

Except for the easy landing on Utah, the first minutes of the assault were generally worse than the leading assault sections had let themselves imagine.

But there were successes as well as failures.

One of them was at Pointe du Hoc, a rocky hundred-foot cliff jutting into the Seine Bay in the eighteen-mile gap between Utah and Omaha. The Germans had a battery of six big guns there. They were 155-millimeter guns in concrete positions,

A German machine gun nest along the Atlantic Wall, background, is captured by Canadian troops on June 8, 1944, following the Allied D-Day invasion. A scaling ladder leans on the massed barbed wire defence to the concrete emplacement.

capable of dominating at least the western half of Omaha and the sea approaches to it.

Two hundred men in a specially trained unit, the Provisional Ranger Force, were to land on the tiny beach at the foot of the cliffs, climb almost straight up, and capture the battery.

The Rangers' commander was Lt. Colonel James E. Rudder, who had been a Texas rancher. When General Bradley first told him what the mission was, the Colonel thought the General was just trying to scare him.

As the Rangers' assault boats neared Pointe du Hoc, the Germans on top of the cliffs came to life. They peppered the small flotilla of LCAs and Ducks (amphibious trucks somewhat like the DD tanks) with artillery and machine-gun fire. That, plus some confusion about direction, made the Rangers forty minutes late.

The destroyer *Saterlee*, seeing why the Rangers were being held up, swept the top of the cliff with fire from all its guns.

But even after the bombardment, one German machine gunner and a number of German rifle men kept the narrow beach hot.

Fifteen of the Rangers were hit as they ran ashore.

Each of the LCAs carried mortars that fired grapnel hooks with ropes and rope ladders attached to them. The mortar crews fired as soon as the LCA's touched down. Many of the hooks, held back by the weight of the wet ropes, failed to shoot over the edge of the cliff. But about a dozen did.

The hooks, like anchors, dug into the flat ground on top. The Rangers, climbing hand over hand, started up the ropes.

But as they were on the way up, Germans arrived directly over their heads and shot down the men who were leading. Then the Germans cut some of the ropes, and slipped one or two off their hooks.

The destroyer *Saterlee* came past again, this time at very close range, firing at the cliff top. Rangers on the beach, aiming well over their companions' heads, picked off some of the Germans when they showed themselves.

In less than five minutes from the time they had hit the beach, the first of the Rangers had crawled over the top. The others swarmed right behind him.

They found an empty tableland, incredibly pockmarked with the craters of bombs and shells. But the concrete gun positions were empty. The big guns had been moved.

The Rangers pushed inland, wiping out several pockets of German resistance as they went. They found the guns in new firing positions in an apple orchard 1,200 yards from the cliff, cleverly camouflaged and with large stores of ammunition nearby. The German gun crews had fled. The Rangers blew up the breeches of the guns (the part that holds the shell in place) with incendiary hand grenades, putting them permanently out of action.

⊚ ⊚ ⊚

For the most part—and especially on Omaha—the first of the assault waves had been stopped in its tracks.

Omaha was the crucial beach, the link between Utah

## ★ NORMANDY TODAY ★

Although visiting them requires a trip to France, the beaches and war memorials at Normandy are among the most well-preserved and maintained historic sites in the world and will remain in your memory forever if you are lucky enough to make the journey. Still visible are many of the German bunkers and trenches, as well as the off-shore jetties built by the Allies to dock their transport ships. Preserved battle equipment, including tanks, landing craft, and artillery pieces,

can be seen in dozens of locations. And the American Cemetery on the bluffs overlooking Omaha beach is the most popular destination of all. More than 9,000 American troops are buried there. For a strikingly different experience, you can also visit La Cambe German Cemetery, located a few miles inland, near Bayeux, France, where 21,000 fallen German soldiers are buried.

There are literally dozens of historic museums and preserved sites

to see in the Normandy area, but one of the most interesting is one described at length in this book: the Pointe du Hoc German artillery installation. Still present at this site are all the German bunker installations, which visitors can climb down into to see the views of the English Channel that German artillery operators must have seen. On high points at the installation, you can still see the large craters where Allied bombs fell in an attempt to destroy the Pointe du Hoc artillery battery.

Though June 6, 1944, was nearly seventy-five years ago, visiting Pointe du Hoc makes the war seem very recent.

on the west and the British beaches on the east. The coast between Utah and Omaha was an eighteen-mile stretch of rock cliff and marsh. The ten miles between Omaha and Gold were all cliff. The troops on Omaha, it was hoped, would move forward at top speed, because the only place the separate landing forces could link together was well inland. Since Omaha was so important, it was the only beach to which two divisions were assigned.

Thirty-four thousand troops and 3,300 vehicles were waiting offshore, in the transport area, to follow the first wave across Omaha. An additional 25,000 men and 4,400 more vehicles were waiting behind *them*. They would be ready to start ashore by noon.

Omaha couldn't fall far behind schedule or the whole intricate plan of the assault would be thrown into a men-and-machines traffic jam on land and sea of disastrous size.

Yet in the half hour that had gone by, the attack had fallen just about half an hour behind time.

Omaha was, physically, a hard beach to cross. Gold, Juno, and Sword were fairly flat, with only low sand dunes between them and the little seaside towns which the Germans had fortified. But Omaha was backed by bluffs a hundred feet high. The American troops had to go uphill to take the German strongpoints.

That was bad enough. But there was another reason why the offensive against Omaha was especially tough. In planning the assault, the Allies had assumed that the Atlantic Wall would be manned by second-rate German troops—men who were older or poorly trained and who would not show much fight in the field. The Allies knew that General Rommel was keeping his first-class field divisions a short distance behind the beaches, ready to move them, when the emergency arose, to wherever they were needed most. One of them, his 352nd Division, was stationed twenty-five miles inland, near the town of St. Lô. The 352nd was expected to counterattack, but the Allies didn't think it could reach the beaches before late in the afternoon of D-Day at the earliest.

But shortly before the invasion fleet sailed, the 352nd had been ordered to move to Omaha to practice anti-landing defense maneuvers.

So this well-trained, seasoned division was right on the bluffs overlooking the beach—exactly where the Germans needed it—when the battle-tried 1st Division and the green but well-trained 29th Division touched down.

◦ ◦ ◦

When the second wave of assault boats reached the beach, starting at seven o'clock, it found that little or nothing had been accomplished.

No one had advanced beyond the beach shingle. Only nine gaps had been blown through the anti-landing obstacles, and three of them were only partial gaps. Just one of these paths was marked, because the Engineers had lost the markers in the surf. They had had a terrible time. Nearly forty percent of them had been killed or wounded.

None of the flamethrower- and demolitions-squad attacks on the Atlantic Wall pillboxes had even started.

A Mulberry harbor was a prefabricated, temporary harbor used when the Allies made a beach landing and had not yet captured a port. This one is assembled in preparation for D-Day, and shows vehicles crossing a floating roadway.

The five beach exits—the only roads off the beach, and the keys to the Omaha effort—were all still held by the enemy.

Gunfire on the beach was as hot as, or even hotter than, it had been at H-Hour. A good many Germans, by now, had rushed to their battle stations, using the network of interconnecting trenches along the bluff top. Others, who had been shaken by the preliminary bombings and shelling, had recovered their senses. Artillery and mortar shells pounded the sand flats. Machine guns and automatic rifles sprayed their fire across the open spaces. Sharpshooters, aiming from the bluffs, were trying to pick off individual soldiers, especially those who had stopped at the water's edge.

And almost all the survivors of the first wave, scattered along the beach shingle, had forgotten about the attack. Their only idea, of necessity, was staying alive.

# CHAPTER ELEVEN

# STANDSTILL

The second wave of assault boats ran into all the same troubles as the first.

One great difficulty was that the boats had been landing and continued to land in the wrong places. Not only was there mist in the air and smoke and dust from the explosions, but the high beach grass that covered the bluffs had caught fire from the shellings. The fog and smoke hid the beach landmarks from the steersmen of the LCVPs. Besides, the current from west to east, on

US Army medical personnel administer a plasma transfusion to a wounded comrade, who survived when his landing craft went down off the coast of Normandy.

account of the storm, was considerably stronger than had been expected. Some of the boats touched down thousands of yards to the left of their marks. Nearly all of them were a few hundred yards too far to the east. And, since each assault section had been briefed so carefully on its specific beach targets, but not on the beach as a whole, a landing error of several hundred yards bewildered the men.

The nine companies in the first wave, according to plan, should have been spaced fairly evenly along Omaha's 7,000 yards. Instead they were jumbled, with boats from one company mixed in with those from another. There were gaps and bunches in the line. Some sections didn't know where they were or where they were supposed to go.

Three boats in the second assault wave, approaching the Vierville draw, met the same sort of reception as A Company, in the first wave. One boat grounded seventy-five yards off shore. As its ramp went down, machine-gun fire beat a tattoo on the bow. Captain Ettore Zappacosta, the company commander, got about ten yards through the water before he was hit twice, in the leg and in the shoulder. "I'm hit!" he yelled.

"Try to make it in!" the medical-aid man, who was still on board the boat, shouted.

But the Captain slumped down and disappeared into the waves. The medical-aid man jumped after him, and was shot and killed before he could get to the spot where the Captain had vanished.

Man by man, every member of the boat section except

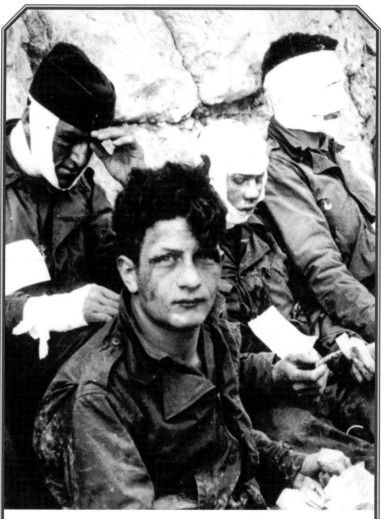

Men of the American assault troops of the 16th Infantry Regiment, injured while storming Omaha Beach during the invasion of Normandy, wait by the chalk cliffs at Collville-sur-Mer for evacuation to a field hospital for further treatment, June 6, 1944.

one was killed or wounded before he reached the beach.

By this time the tide was coming in very fast. It advanced eight feet in the half-hour between 7:00 and 7:30. It was beginning to wash up a line of the dead, along with wrecked pieces of equipment, especially hundreds of inflated twin-tube life preservers. Many of the wounded, unable to crawl faster than the tide's progress, had drowned in the surge of the surf. It was a terrible time in which men, driven out of their wits, did strange, desperate things. One wounded man, part way across the sands, lay hugging a live mine. A life preserver had gotten wrapped around it, and perhaps it was the life preserver he was clutching. In any case, his companions tried to tell him what he was doing, but he wouldn't pay any attention. They couldn't loosen his firm grip on the deadly explosive charge.

* * *

At 7:30—a full hour after H-Hour—the assault on Omaha beach was at a standstill. A great many men had died. Those who were alive, for the most part, looked dead. Most of the living were lying on the shingle behind a low wooden-and-concrete sea wall that had been built to protect the road along the beach from the waves at high tide. The wall was about two-thirds of the way in from the water to the foot of the bluffs, and it was three or four feet high. It gave some protection—although not enough—from the steady rain of German gunfire.

But the Americans behind the wall were paralyzed by something worse than fear of being hit by a bullet or a fragment of a German shell. They were in a state of shock, like people who have been in a bad accident. They were numb and dazed. Many of them could hardly move at all. They realized vaguely that they were in danger behind the sea wall, and that German artillery and mortar shells could easily hit them. Even so—even knowing the peril of where they were, and seeing that there was less danger at the foot of the bluffs where they could take cover and hide—they were too stunned to act. The cold, their seasickness, the frightful experience of seeing their fellow soldiers shot down, all led to a numbing paralysis. Worst of all, many of the men thought the invasion had failed. The plan was so badly scrambled that it seemed impossible the attack could ever move forward.

The assault had achieved less in the first hour than was expected of it in the first five minutes.

# CHAPTER TWELVE

# FIRST ON HIGH GROUND

The miraculous part of the story, as the military historians later found out, was how the attack got started again.

In the crisis, a handful of heroes came forward. They were men who decided that, however hopeless the battle seemed, they themselves would try to do something. Any action, they thought, was better than none. Each man, at the moment of his heroic decision, acted alone. It might have been easier for him if he had known there were others like him at other places along the beach, but none

A tribute to an unknown American soldier, who lost his life fighting in the landing operations of the Allied Forces, marks the sand of Normandy's shore, in June 1944.

of them did. They only knew that, where they were, the attack was stalled. Each man decided, independently, to do his best whether or not, in the long run, his best could make much difference.

⊙　⊙　⊙

One such man was 1st Lieutenant William D. Moody, an officer in C Company of the 2nd Ranger Battalion. He belonged to the outfit that was knocking out the German guns at Pointe du Hoc. But his particular company had another gun battery, closer to Vierville, as its target. The guns were at a place called Pointe de la Percée, some 2,000 yards west of the Vierville draw. They had to be approached from the side.

Moody and sixty-three other C Company Rangers, in two LCAs, had come in with the first wave of assault boats. They were headed for the beach a short distance west of Vierville, where the sands narrowed and the bluffs became rocky cliffs.

A German anti-tank gun, shooting from the top of the bluffs, dropped two shells into the water right beside the boat in which C Company's commander, Captain Ralph Goranson, was riding. The shells exploded when they hit the water. Twelve of the section's thirty-two men were killed and several others were wounded. But both LCAs kept going until they grounded on a sand bar under the water.

Although they were still some distance off shore, the LCAs at once lowered their ramps. And right away, German machine-gun fire started to sizzle around them. As the men pushed forward to get out, bullets raked the ramps and the water just in front of them in deadly accurate bursts. Lieutenant Moody and his men stepped off their ramp into water up to their necks. It is impossible to walk fast in neck-deep surf, and the Rangers had to walk, not swim, because they were holding their rifles high over their heads to keep them dry. It took all their strength to inch forward. The German marksmen, their aim helped by the Rangers' slowness, hit fifteen of the thirty-two men from Moody's boat as they struggled toward the shore.

It was about 250 yards from the edge of the water and across the sand to the base of the cliffs. A few of the Rangers made the mistake of crouching in the water or lying at its edge. Most of them were soon hit.

The men who headed for the base of the cliffs discovered how weak they were after pushing through the water. It took the fastest of them three or four minutes to walk the distance. (They should have been able to run it in less than a minute.) The slowest, including some men who were wounded but were able to move, crawled across the beach. Their dark olive-drab uniforms, made darker by being soaking wet, contrasted sharply with the light-colored sand. That made them excellent targets for the German gunners and mortar crews. Just twenty-nine of C Company's sixty-four men got all the way to the foot of the cliffs.

The cliffs, at this point, were nearly vertical and about ninety feet tall. The sea had hollowed out caves at their base. As long as C Company's survivors stayed close to the rocky

US infantry patrol picking its way through the blasted ruins of Saint-Lô. The Germans destroyed most of the town before the Allies recaptured it on July 18, 1944.

wall, they were out of the range of the enemy's fire. Most of the twenty-nine men were content to stay where they were. They were too worn out, physically and mentally, to do anything more.

But Lieutenant Moody, who had been through as much as anyone else and had the same reasons for feeling hopeless, wanted to keep going.

Moody could see that the remnant of C Company couldn't climb the sheer wall of rock where they were. He decided to try to find a better place. To carry out his plan, though, he would need help. He looked over the bedraggled bunch of Rangers and picked out two men. He told them to follow him, and all three picked their way to the west, staying close to the cliffs, for about three hundred yards. All of them carried ropes and stakes, which were part of the Rangers' special equipment.

Finally Moody spotted a crevice in the cliff that ran from the bottom all the way to the top. It looked like a possible way up the rocks—if there were no Germans waiting for the climbers at the top.

Moody reached up and rammed his bayonet into the crack in the rocks. He tested it with a pull to see if it was firm enough to support his weight. It was. With a handhold on the bayonet, he scrambled up the face of the cliff a little way. The two other men followed him. Up the crevice they worked their way, jabbing in their bayonets for successive handholds or toeholds in places where they couldn't find any on the rock itself, and pulling each other along until they were within about fifteen feet of the top..

From there on the cliff receded sharply, so that climbing would have been comparatively easy except for one factor. The Germans had planted land mines. They were saucer-shaped discs filled with high explosive and buried in the ground. They would go off under very little pressure—if, for instance, a man stepped on one or crawled over it. Despite the mines, the three-man party advanced cautiously onto the slope, gingerly probing the ground with their bayonets before putting their weight on it. Then they drove their stakes into the ground, and fastened four toggle ropes to the stakes, letting the loose ends hang down the cliff beside the crevice. The ropes had short crosspieces of wood, or toggles, attached every few feet, making a ladder of extremely simple design.

While Moody and his two Rangers were working on the ropes, with the idea that the rest of C Company would be able to follow them up the cliff, a splattering of rifle fire landed pretty close by. The three men hit the ground and waited. There was another burst, wilder than the first. The shots were coming from the east, from somewhere near Vierville. Moody left one of his men at the stakes to guard the ropes. He and the other man then worked east along the top of the cliffs, taking every possible advantage of the uneven ground and the brush to keep out of sight. They suspected, without being able to see anything clearly, that the Germans who had shot at them were in a large, barnlike stone building six or seven hundred yards away. Halfway to it, they came to the place on the top of the cliff that was directly above where C Company's other men, with Captain Goranson, were waiting. Moody shouted down and gave them directions to the crevice and the four ropes.

Then it was perfectly obvious to the rest of the Rangers that the cliffs could be scaled. For there was Lieutenant Moody, all in one piece and as big as life, explaining how he and the other two men had done it. Captain Goranson led the twenty-five men to the ropes along the route Moody's party had reconnoitered. In short order, they all monkey-walked to the top like mountain climbers, using the toggles on the ropes for hand holds, leaning back with most of their weight on their arms, and with their feet braced against the face of the rock.

By about 7:30 all twenty-nine of the men were on top of the cliff and preparing to move east, in Moody's footsteps, to attack the fortified stone barn. That gave C Company—what there was left of it, at least—the honor of being the first unit in the Omaha assault to reach high ground.

# ★ ALLIED FIGHTER PLANES ★

**Allied fighter aircraft performed three crucial missions during the invasion: providing air support for the ground troops, protecting Allied bombers and transport planes from attacks by German interceptors, and keeping the planes of the German air force, or Luftwaffe, away from the landing beaches Here are four fighters that played key roles in the success of the invasion.**

## HAWKER TYPHOON

Designed by famed British aeronautical engineer Sydney Camm, the Typhoon entered combat service with Britain's Royal Air Force (RAF) in 1941. Although conceived as a medium- to high-altitude interceptor, the Typhoon was ultimately employed mostly as a fighter-bomber, attacking enemy installations, vehicles, and troop positions. Fast, powerful, and heavily armed with four Hispano 20mm cannons and either bombs or rockets, the Typhoon became one of the most effective ground-attack aircraft of World War II. Eighteen squadrons of Typhoons with the RAF's Second Tactical Air Force were available to the Allies on D-Day,

and over the following weeks they were heavily engaged in supporting the Allied invasion troops and blunting German counterattacks. Notwithstanding its effectiveness, the Typhoon was troubled by problems with its airframe and engine, leading Camm and Hawker Aircraft to develop its successor, the Hawker Tempest.

In this photo, a Hawker Typhoon is serviced and armed by an RAF ground crew, June 1944. Note the rockets being loaded onto the launch racks under the wings. The black and white stripes visible on the wings were applied to Allied aircraft just before D-Day to facilitate easy identification of friendly planes.

## NORTH AMERICAN P-51 MUSTANG

North American Aviation developed the P-51 Mustang from drawing board to prototype in just 102 days in response to a British request. Powered by an American-made Allison engine, the Mustang was initially employed by the RAF primarily as a fast reconnaissance aircraft and fighter-bomber. Later, however, after being re-equipped with a British-designed Rolls Royce Merlin engine built by Packard, the Mustang found its place in history as a long-range, high-performance fighter that excelled as an escort for American bombers attacking strategic targets deep in enemy territory. Deployed from England with the US Eighth and Ninth Air Forces, Mustangs were a key enforcer of Allied air superiority during the Normandy invasion. Two decades after the end of the war, the Ford Motor Company named its Mustang automobile in honor of the P-51.

In the photo above P-51 Mustangs of the US 361st Fighter Group, Eighth Air Force, fly over England in 1944 after the Normandy invasion. The nearest three planes are the P-51D model, equipped with a "bubble" canopy to improve pilot visibility. The farthest aircraft is an older P-51B. All the planes are carrying external fuel tanks under the wings and are painted with black and white invasion stripes.

## SUPERMARINE SPITFIRE

Designed by R. J. Mitchell of Supermarine Aviation Works based in part on earlier Supermarine racing planes, the Spitfire made its flight debut in 1936. It was soon ordered by the RAF as a high-performance interceptor, and in 1940 it proved itself against the Luftwaffe in the Battle of Britain. Continually refined and updated during its long operational life, the Spitfire was the RAF's premier fighter aircraft throughout World War II. It also equipped many US Army Air Force (USAAF) and Royal Canadian Air Force (RCAF) squadrons. Renowned for its combination of speed and maneuverability, the Spitfire was a tough opponent for German Messerschmitt Bf 109 and Focke-Wulf Fw 190 fighters, and it

helped ensure that the D-Day invasion forces would be protected from Luftwaffe air attacks. In July 1944, a few weeks after the invasion, an RCAF Spitfire strafed a staff car in which the German commander in Normandy, Field Marshal Erwin Rommel, was riding. Rommel, injured in the attack, was still convalescing when, on October 14, he was forced to commit suicide after being implicated in a plot to assassinate Adolf Hitler.

This is the Spitfire Mk IX, introduced in 1942 in response to the German introduction of the formidable Focke-Wulf Fw 190. Featuring an upgraded Rolls Royce Merlin engine, the Spitfire Mk IX was the backbone of the RAF's fighter squadrons during the middle years of the war.

## REPUBLIC P-47 THUNDERBOLT

Nicknamed the "Jug" by its pilots, the big Republic P-47 Thunderbolt was the first USAAF fighter aircraft to reach Great Britain in numbers after the American entry into the war. Powerful, tough, and heavily armed with eight .50 caliber machine guns, the P-47 initially saw service with the Eighth Air Force primarily as an escort for US strategic bombers, and it bore the brunt of the Americans' fight against Luftwaffe interceptors in 1943 and early 1944. In the months after the Normandy invasion, P-47s of the US Ninth Air Force, then stationed at airfields captured by the Allies on the European continent, excelled as fighter-bombers providing close support for Allied troops battling their way into the heart of the Third Reich.

Above, P-47 Thunderbolts are serviced at an airfield in France after D-Day. Note the distinctive black and white invasion stripes on the wings and fuselage.

## • CHAPTER THIRTEEN •

# LAMBERT WOULD TRY

About a mile farther to the east, there was another young man who, like Moody, wouldn't be stopped. He was Private Ingram E. Lambert. He belonged to another C Company, this one an infantry outfit, part of the 116th Regiment. According to plan, Lambert's unit, in six boats, should have touched down in front of Vierville at 7:20. It was in the second wave. The men expected to finish up whatever the first wave had left undone in clearing the exit from the beach onto the Vierville road.

An American soldier, tired and dirty from advancing the front after the D-Day invasion.

The boats actually landed a thousand or more yards east of where they were supposed to be. Haze and smoke hung over the landscape, hiding almost everything, including the town of Vierville. Lambert and the other men in his company were unable to recognize any of the landmarks they had memorized from maps. They weren't sure where they were. As they came in close, about all they could see on the beach were several DD tanks. It was hard to tell whether the tanks were still working. There were no signs of the first-wave troops that were supposed to have crossed the beach ahead of them. In fact, the beach looked very much as if no one except the tank crews had been on it during the first fifty minutes. That was precisely the case. Lambert's company was the first unit ashore at that particular place.

On the other hand, being in the wrong place had its advantages. The German defenses here were quieter than those near Vierville. If Lambert's outfit had landed where it should have, it certainly would have met the same shattering fire as the Rangers and A Company of the 116th. Here the shellfire from the shore was light. One of the six LCVPs tipped over close to the shore, spilling men and equipment into the water, but it was shallow enough that the men could wade ashore. The loss in equipment—flamethrowers, explosive charges, and mortars—was the most serious part of the accident.

Like the other men in his company, Lambert was amazed, when he waded out of the surf onto the sand, to find that the great preliminary air bombardment had not hit the beach.

The infantrymen had counted on finding the sandy flats pockmarked with shallow bomb craters. They had expected to cross the beach by running from one hole to the next, hiding in them from German fire. There were no such craters. The flats were almost as slick as they could be. It was a frightening disappointment.

But even though the beach defenses hadn't been damaged, Lambert's company got across the open stretch of sand to the sea wall in good order, with only five or six casualties on the way. The men's weapons were mostly dry, ready to shoot. The unit kept together and was not, like so many others, scattered all over the place.

In fact, C Company's landing was about as good as any outfit's all along the beach. Unfortunately Lambert and the others didn't know that they were doing well. As far as they could see (which wasn't far on account of the grass fires' smoke), they were all alone. The troops that were supposed to have come in ahead of them seemed to have vanished.

Men who have been in combat awhile gradually get used to the surprising emptiness of a battlefield. A front line is likely to look completely deserted unless the terrain is studied most carefully. Naturally, no soldier makes himself any more of a target than he has to. He doesn't draw the enemy's attention to himself by moving unless he has to, and then he usually crawls, close to the ground. So small units have to learn that they have not necessarily been abandoned, even when they can't see anybody else. Because C Company was in action for the first time, they had not learned this. They felt as if the great assault had been called off and someone had forgotten to tell them.

For fifteen or twenty minutes no one did anything. The men lay low behind the sea wall, trying to keep out of the way of the German rifle and mortar fire, just taking stock of the situation.

At 7:50, Lambert decided that someone had to get something going, and that he would be the man to try it. Behind the sea wall, there was the narrow beach road. In happier times, summer vacationists had used it as a promenade. Now the Germans had strung barbed wire along its inland edge, making a barrier in the way of C Company's advance. Behind the wire was a swampy, flat stretch of about 150 yards to the base of the grassy bluffs. The problem was to blow a hole in the barbed wire. It was not an easy task. The Germans on the bluffs were keeping the promenade well sprinkled with rifle fire and occasional light artillery and mortar fire.

Lambert picked up a bangalore torpedo, a high-explosive charge in a long pipe-like casing especially designed for blasting a path through minefields or barbed wire. He crawled over the sea wall, carrying the bangalore. He ran the few steps to the far side of the road, shoved the long demolition charge under the wire, and pulled the device that was supposed to set it off, a friction igniter.

Then he threw himself onto the ground, with his arms over his head, waiting for the blast of the explosion. But the bangalore did not go off. Before Lambert could do anything about the failure, a burst of shots from a machine gun hit him, killing him instantly.

Lambert died without knowing how important his effort, which took only a few seconds, was going to prove. The moment Lambert was hit, his platoon leader, 2nd Lieutenant Stanley M. Schwartz, jumped in to take his place. Schwartz darted across the road. Kneeling close to Lambert's dead body, he set about to make the igniter work. On the second pull, it set off the bangalore. In a matter of minutes, C Company was on the move.

The first soldier who dashed across the road and through the hole in the wire was shot down. But the next man made it safely and dove into an abandoned trench behind the wire. Others rushed through close behind him.

The Germans on the bluffs turned machine guns on the gap Lambert and Schwartz had blown. Then they tried to close the opening with artillery fire. But they were too late. After about ten minutes—the time it took for a small group to form in the trench—C Company went on with its advance. The men started for the bluffs, running a short way and then dropping to the ground, taking cover in clumps of grass or behind bushes.

Once they had reached the rising slope of the bluffs, they were protected by the folds of the ground and hidden by the drifting smoke. A second gap in the wire had been cut shortly after the first had been blown. Two groups of men combined and moved up the hill. They advanced in a narrow column, keeping a sharp lookout for signs that the ground had been mined. They found that the German trenches on the top of the bluff had been abandoned, so they kept right on going for about two hundred yards into some flat, open fields. There German machine-gun fire came at them from both sides. C Company halted. But its advance that far, which Lambert had started, was the first real break we made in the German line.

# CHAPTER FOURTEEN

# INFANTRYMEN NOW

About half a mile farther east, there was a small seaside village called Les Moulins. It had been strongly fortified, and the Germans were ready and waiting to keep the invaders from using the road that ran inland from the beach to the town. Six boats carrying the men of F Company of the 116th Regiment landed near Les Moulins. The three boats on the west made out better than the three on the east because the grass fires' smoke—the same smoke that had helped Lambert—hid them. But the three boats on the east took the full fury of German fire. For forty-five minutes, the

American artillery forward observers.

infantrymen struggled to get across the sandy stretch from the water's edge to the sea wall, and only half of them made it. Those who did were too badly shaken to continue the attack. The three western sections of F Company lost fewer men, but many of those they did lose were officers and top-ranking non-commissioned officers. They were badly disorganized by the time they reached the sea wall.

While the first sections of F Company were still moving across the sands, the boats containing battalion headquarters came in. The battalion commander, major Sidney V. Bingham Jr., got to the road almost as soon as his leading assault troops. He set right to work trying to revive a fighting spirit in the leaderless men, and to find out what had happened to his scattered battalion. None of the radios that had come in with his headquarters company was working. That made it impossible for the major to get any information or give any orders to the battalion as a whole.

But while Major Bingham couldn't organize a strong attack against Les Moulins, he did manage to lead a small force of about fifty men off the beach and into a network of abandoned German trenches near a tall, three-story house at the mouth of the Les Moulins draw. It was a feeble effort compared to the attack that had been planned and rehearsed. But even a feeble effort, on a beach that was filling with men too shocked and dazed to try anything at all, was worth a great deal.

One of the officers helping Major Bingham had been wounded. A shell fragment had gone through both his cheeks. Whenever he talked, urging men to get up and go, blood spouted from his mouth. But the officer seemed determined to ignore it, and that made his suggestions all the more impressive.

One trouble with Bingham's little group, besides its being too small and made up of assorted men from various units, was lack of fire power. Many of the men's rifles were clogged with sand. They jammed or missed fire often enough to rob the force of as much power as fifty soldiers should have had.

The major tried hard, with a squad of ten, to work his way up the bluff and knock out a machine-gun nest that was causing much of the horror on the sands. He got close to the machine-gun emplacement, but couldn't take it. There was nothing to do but retreat to the trenches near the house and try to build up more strength.

At about half-past eight, while Major Bingham was still trying to silence the machine-gun nest, an advance party of his supporting artillery landed. They were forward observers, liaison parties, and communications specialists of the 111th Field Artillery Battalion, the regular partners in combat of the 116th Infantry Regiment. (Forward observers, during an ordinary battle, are placed up front with the infantry to find out where artillery fire is needed to help them. The observers telephone back to the guns, which then provide it as quickly and accurately as they can.)

This advance party was much too early. Its 105-millimeter howitzers were to land later. They would be used in the drive inland from the top of the bluffs. So far the infantry hadn't made much progress off the beach.

As the landing boat in which he was riding approached Les Moulins, the artillery battalion commander, Lieutenant-Colonel Thornton L. Mullins, could see through his field glasses that Bingham's battalion was in trouble. He saw that the invasion's schedule had been too hopeful, and that the first waves, instead of having charged over the bluffs, were just hanging onto the sea wall.

Colonel Mullins' first thought, when he realized what had happened on the shore, was that he would do what he could, and ignore the fact that the plan had gone all wrong.

Mullins' staff intelligence officer, Lieutenant Richard Brush, was standing in the boat beside him.

"Never mind our artillery mission," Mullins said to him. "We've got to be infantrymen now."

The artillerymen stepped off their boat into water up around their waists. They plodded in toward the sandy flats trying not to pay too much attention to the German bullets that zipped around them. One bullet nicked Colonel Mullins' upper arm, cutting the flesh. He ignored the wound.

At the sea wall, he found the mixture of men from several different units dazed and bewildered. Many of them, Colonel Mullins noticed, had dropped or thrown away their rifles or carbines. His first idea was to persuade the men, one at a time, to find something to shoot and to start shooting back. The beach was littered with equipment and weapons of every kind. While it seems strange that soldiers would need to be told to pick up guns, it was just what they did need. They were so stunned they needed to be started on the simplest acts.

An American soldier firing a bazooka over a hedgerow.

A German pillbox on Utah Beach, captured by the Allies.

The colonel crawled along, trying to keep down behind the sea wall, urging the infantrymen to snap out of their daze. He showed some men rifles that were theirs for the picking up. He started others cleaning the wet sand out of the barrels and chambers of their weapons so they could shoot with them. The men began to come alive again and to realize that there was no sense in lying helplessly on the beach.

While he was in the midst of this job, Colonel Mullins was hit a second time. A rifle bullet went through his hand. He kept right on going.

A pair of DD tanks caught his attention. They were both firing their guns doggedly, but they didn't seem to be firing at any particular targets. Colonel Mullins thought he could improve their aim. He wanted to get them pointed at the Les Moulins pillboxes, for he knew that the infantry at the mouth of the draw was badly in need of help. He left the sea wall and walked back onto the sand flats where there was no protection at all against enemy fire. While the colonel, like a parking-lot attendant signaling an automobile driver where to park, waved directions, one of the tanks shifted position. The colonel pointed out one of the emplacements near the top of the Les Moulins draw. The tank's gun fired. Smoke and a shower of dirt flew into the air from what looked like a direct hit.

Colonel Mullins thought he saw a better beach position for the second tank. It was a few yards farther along. In order to make sure that the sand wasn't mined, he walked ahead of the tank, studying the beach. The tank, with its powerful engine roaring, got set to follow. But before it could do so, the Colonel was wounded for the third time. He was hit in the stomach. This time—although there was still so much to be done—he couldn't ignore it. Colonel Mullins fell forward, dead.

# CHAPTER FIFTEEN

# SHUFORD AND THE CHIEF

It was just as well that Colonel Mullins, before he was killed, and the others in the advance party of the 111th Field Artillery Battalion didn't know what was happening to the battalion's twelve howitzers. The news was all bad.

The forward observers and liaison officers on the beach assumed that the guns would be ready to come ashore as soon as their gunners were told, by radio, that the beach exits were clear. It never crossed their minds—not, at least, until hours later—that the artillery was in almost as much trouble as the infantry.

**Top:** German artillery. **Bottom:** American soldiers firing a howitzer.

Each of the guns was loaded on an amphibious truck, a combination boat and automobile colloquially known as a "Duck." The DUKW were supposed to sail in under their own power, drive out of the surf onto the sand on their wheels, and then go to the first gun positions. If the weather had been slightly better and the sea a little less choppy, they might have been able to do so.

The battalion filled thirteen Ducks. There was one for each howitzer and an extra one for battalion headquarters. Things had begun to go wrong hours before H-Hour, as soon as the Ducks were launched from the big LSTs that had brought them across the Channel. The LSTs were anchored some seven miles off the beach. At 2:00 a.m., when it was very dark, the first Duck had rolled out of its LSTs open bow and down a steel ramp toward the water. She had slid off the ramp into the sea, burying her nose in a wave. Her stern had settled down with a clumsy squish. Right away it was clear that she was overloaded. The choppy, four-foot waves, slapping against her sides, were sloshing a dangerous amount of water aboard. The weight of the howitzer, by itself, was considerable. And, in addition, the Duck was carrying thirteen artillerymen, fifty shells, and other equipment a gun crew uses: a radio, telephones and wire, picks and shovels, a camouflage net with its twelve steel support poles, sandbags, K-rations (packages of concentrated food that can be eaten without cooking), and the cannoneers' knapsacks, called musette bags, filled with their personal belongings.

Two of the thirteen Ducks sank minutes after they were launched. One of them, caught by the current, was washed back against the LST's ramp, crashed heavily against it, and went down like a stone. The cannoneers, in their inflated life belts, were picked up, but the howitzer was gone forever. The second Duck stayed afloat only a little longer. Then a wave hit her at a bad angle. She rolled partly over, took more water aboard, and went down.

The remaining ten, with the Headquarters Duck, headed for a stretch of water about six hundred yards from the LST. They were supposed to wait there, moving slowly around in a large circle, until they got word from the beach that it was time to come ashore.

Three more of the Ducks, including the Headquarters Duck, sank on the way to this rendezvous area. Their story was much the same: They took water aboard faster than the automatic pumps could get rid of it.

Two more went down as they tried to circle, waiting to hear from the advance party. That left only six guns. Half the 111th's fire power was lost, and the long run into Omaha beach was still to come. The situation was so bad that the artillerymen in the six Ducks that were still afloat couldn't quite believe it. Their whole effort for a year had been devoted to getting ready for this action. No one had dreamed that half the battalion's guns would wind up on the bottom of the Channel seven miles from shore.

After a long wait for word from the beach, which didn't come, the six Ducks started in. A Navy LCVP, acting as guide and navigator, led the procession. They had gone only a few hundred yards, moving at full speed ahead, when the waves swamped two more of the Ducks.

The other four kept going toward Les Moulins.

In the first of the four, close behind the navy guide boat, was Captain Louis A. Shuford. He was the commanding officer of C Battery, which had only two howitzers left. The second one was in the Duck behind Shuford's. Captain Jack Wilson of A Battery, who had only one of his four guns left, was in charge of the third Duck. The fourth and last in line contained B Battery's one remaining gun.

Shuford was twenty-five years old, good natured, and quiet in manner. He had been born and brought up in Virginia and had been a track star at Fork Union Military Academy and at Richmond University. The men in his battery had nicknamed him "Boobytrap" because he was fascinated by explosives and explosive devices and spent a lot of time experimenting with them as a hobby. Shuford's superior officers rated him as a good but not perfect battery commander. He hated the paperwork his job required, and he had often been in trouble with Colonel Mullins because his records were not up to date. It is safe to say that no one, including Shuford, expected that he was going to be a hero.

While the four guns were still several thousand yards away from Omaha beach, the second Duck in line, behind Shuford's, began to sink. Shuford thought he might be able to save it by lightening its load. He signaled to the coxswain in the navy guide boat, and the LCVP took off twelve of the thirteen artillerymen. The Duck was still pretty low in the water, but with about two thousand pounds less to carry it, stopped going down.

The navy LCVP headed back out to sea, looking for a larger boat or a rhino-ferry (one of the huge rafts that were bringing in heavy equipment) on which it might deposit the cannoneers.

The four Ducks kept on going without their guide boat. At about one thousand yards from the shore, where the boat traffic was fairly heavy with LCAs, LCVPs, and other small boats, they lost each other for a while. The crewless Duck, with just its gun, one artilleryman, and its driver aboard, developed engine trouble. While it was stalled, a splatter of long-range machine-gun fire from the bluff tore open one of its sides. That finished it. More water poured into the hold, and down it went. A few minutes later the last Duck in the procession, B Battery's, filled and sank.

By this time it was about nine o'clock, and the 111th Field Artillery Battalion had only two howitzers left. Shuford and Wilson maneuvered their Ducks alongside each other, and lashed them together with rope. Then the two battery commanders had a conference. They were desperate. They were five or six hundred yards offshore and they could see that the Ducks couldn't go any closer. They didn't know what had happened to the first waves of the infantry, or to their own battalion's advance party, but they could see bursts of German mortar and artillery shells exploding on the sand flats. Knowing that they were all that remained of the 111th,

American soldiers with a French tank, recaptured from the Germans who had been using it.

and realizing that the attack was hours behind schedule, the two captains couldn't help feeling that the great assault had turned into a disaster.

While they talked, the other men in the Ducks crouched low. German bullets and shell fragments were whining past. The hulls of the Ducks, though thin, offered some protection. The men were drenched with spray and they were cold, even though the sun was beginning to come through the haze and smoke that lay over the seascape. And, after six hours of riding in rough waters, they were seasick.

Shuford and Wilson agreed that even though the invasion looked hopeless, they ought to try to get ashore.

They thought they could roll onto the beach and start shooting. They would use the hoisting device on Shuford's Duck to lift Wilson's howitzer out of the hold of its Duck. Then Wilson's hoist would be used to lift Shuford's gun.

"We might as well try it," Captain Wilson said. "We ought to be able to knock out at least one pillbox."

But even this simple plan was too ambitious.

A burst of machine-gun fire peppered the two Ducks with lead and cut the rope holding them together. Shuford's pulled ahead, trying to get out of range. But one of the bullets had hit the engine of Wilson's Duck, disabling it. While the craft drifted helplessly, a second flurry of bullets hit it, wounding several of the men. Then a light artillery shell hit the breech block of the howitzer, putting it out of commission for good. The shell fragments killed one man and wounded a few more. Finally, the Duck caught fire. Wilson ordered his men to jump overboard and jumped with them.

When Shuford realized that Wilson's Duck had been hit, he started back to help, but a large assault boat, an LCI (Landing Craft, Infantry), blocked his way. By the time it passed, Shuford couldn't see what had become of Wilson, the Duck, or the gun crew. Suddenly a German gun began shooting at Shuford's Duck. One shell sent up a geyser of water just ahead of it. The next landed just behind. Shuford ordered his Duck driver to head out to sea at full speed.

The gun crew in Shuford's Duck had named their gun "The Chief," and had painted a handsome picture of an Indian chief on its shield. The Chief was the only gun the 111th Field Artillery Battalion had left. It represented the last chance for the battalion to play a part in the assault. This fact strengthened Shuford's determination to get the gun ashore. Without Wilson's hoist, though, he did not know how he would go about unloading it.

But he had several problems to solve before he could unload. His Duck was now leaking pretty badly from the holes the machine-gun fire had drilled in its hull. It looked as if it couldn't stay afloat much longer. But Shuford had no information about where he could land.

He thought the navy might give him some advice. It was supposed to be in touch by radio with the artillery's advance parties and with its own shore parties which directed naval gunfire.

Shuford headed for the nearest large ship, an LCI like the one that had cut him off when he had been searching for

Wilson. As his Duck came alongside the LCI, his driver said, "You'd better hurry, Captain. I don't think this thing is going to hold together much longer."

Shuford scrambled aboard the LCI.

The navy's radio network was working, just as Shuford hoped, but the news from the beach was bad. Lieutenant Brush, who was still near the Les Moulins draw, reported that the beach there, called Easy Green, was not yet clear. His message suggested that Shuford try Fox, the next beach section to the east of Les Moulins.

The radio operator called the forward observers on Fox. Things were just as bad there. "Don't come to Fox," Fox warned. "Go to Easy Green."

That left Shuford no better off than he had been, except that he knew two places where he couldn't get ashore. By now it was nearly 11 o'clock, and much warmer, but the men in the Duck were too numb with discouragement to notice the improvement. Everyone was quiet—most unusual for twelve cannoneers. The Duck driver was the only one with much to say. He kept repeating what was clearly true: It wouldn't be long before the Duck would sink. For a time the Duck circled aimlessly while the men took turns at the hand pump. Shuford again tried to call the shore with a navy radio, but the news remained bad. None of the beaches was open.

Shuford decided that the only way he could keep afloat was by tying up to one of the rhino-ferries that were waiting, like him, for a place to go ashore. By luck, the one he picked carried some of the 111th's jeeps and trucks and the men of the battalion who made up part of its reserve. They didn't know what had happened to the other eleven guns, or realize that the first waves of infantry were still battling for the beach exits. And Shuford and his men were too exhausted to tell them. They lashed the Duck to the raft, leaving only its driver on board. Then they crawled onto the ferry's flat deck, stretched out wherever they could find space, and fell asleep.

It was more like a collapse than ordinary sleep. And it didn't last long. Shuford was awakened by the Duck driver, shaking him and shouting that the Duck was sinking.

The Duck was filling faster than ever. The water was slapping around the Chief's big rubber tires. There was no way of getting the gun out of the Duck and onto the rhino-ferry without a good-sized crane.

Shuford spotted just such a crane on another rhino-ferry five or six hundred yards away. He doubted the Duck could get that far. But he was going to lose the Chief anyhow, so it seemed worth a try. All hands pitched in to unload the equipment—everything except the Chief—from the Duck, cutting the weight down to a minimum. Shuford decided that one man, besides the driver and himself, would be needed on the short run, to help bail water. Off they set, with the Duck riding so low in the water that a single wave sloshing aboard could have sent her to the bottom.

But she made it. Shuford jumped onto the second rhino-ferry, shouting for help. A lieutenant-colonel was in charge. He thought Shuford was out of his mind. What was so important, he wanted to know, about one stray howitzer?

And a howitzer without a gun crew, at that?

It was a question Shuford couldn't really answer. Instead of trying, he lost his temper and yelled at the lieutenant-colonel.

The lieutenant-colonel was horrified. He didn't have the faintest idea what the Chief meant to Shuford. Still, he was impressed by Shuford's wild insistence, and he himself operated the crane. The Chief was swung up out of the Duck and deposited on the deck of the ferry.

After the Chief was safely aboard, Shuford discovered that the ferry was bringing in parts of the 7th Field Artillery Battalion. The 7th's job exactly matched the 111th's. It was supposed to be supporting the 16th Infantry, and, like the 111th, it had been having a hard time. Six of its twelve guns had already gone down.

At last Shuford had the answer to his problem. The 7th Battalion needed the Chief, so he presented his gun to one of the 7th's officers. Late in the afternoon, the Chief went ashore with a 7th Battalion battery. Before midnight, she was in firing position, pouring high explosives into Normandy in support of the infantry's slow but all-important advance.

Shuford's wish had come true. Part of the 111th—even if only one gun, and a gun that another outfit had to operate— was helping the assault succeed.

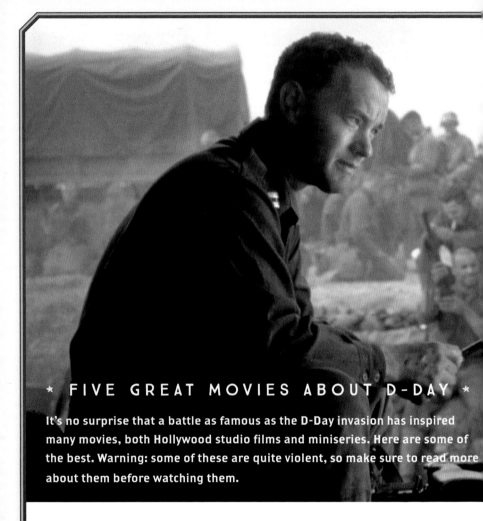

## ★ FIVE GREAT MOVIES ABOUT D-DAY ★

It's no surprise that a battle as famous as the **D-Day** invasion has inspired many movies, both Hollywood studio films and miniseries. Here are some of the best. Warning: some of these are quite violent, so make sure to read more about them before watching them.

### SAVING PRIVATE RYAN (1998)

This movie from Steven Spielberg depicts the D-Day landing, then follows a group of US soldiers as they go behind enemy lines to retrieve a soldier whose brothers have been killed in battle. This movie stars Tom Hanks and Matt Damon and won five Academy Awards, though not best picture. It is one of the very best movies on the subject but is extremely violent. Pictured above.

### THE LONGEST DAY (1962)

This black-and-white movie tells the story of D-Day from both the American and German points of view. It features an all-star cast with some of the most famous actors of the day, including Henry Fonda, John Wayne, Robert Mitchum, and Sean Connery. It won the Academy Award for best picture.

## BAND OF BROTHERS (2001)

This excellent miniseries does take some time to watch in its entirety. It tells the story of a parachute infantry regiment from basic training all the way until the end of the war, including the D-Day invasion and the Battle of the Bulge. Its actors are not well-known, but of all the movies about the European war, this could be the best.

## THE BIG RED ONE (1980)

This movie follows an infantry division led by Lee Marvin from battles in North Africa and Sicily through to D-Day. It also stars a young Mark Hamill (the future Luke Skywalker) as a private.

## OVERLORD (1975)

This is a British view of D-Day as seen through the eyes of one young soldier. It stands out because it includes archival footage of the actual battle.

• CHAPTER SIXTEEN •

# DAWSON'S GOOD
# THROW

Captain Joseph T. Dawson commanded Company G of the 16th Regiment, which came in between the Les Moulins and Colleville draws. Company G, which landed at seven o'clock, thought it was part of the second assault wave, until it discovered that it had the first wave's job to do.

Five of its six assault boats touched down together on time and in the right place. They followed three assault boats from two other companies which had crossed the sand flats safely, but were having trouble, when they reached the base of the bluffs, with German rifle fire.

**Top:** The crew of an American landing craft that struck a mine and sank are helped ashore on the western end of Omaha beach by army engineers and other personnel. **Bottom:** A German paratroop mortar crew aims to stop the Allied advance on Saint-Lô.

By the time Dawson's men waded out of the surf and started across the beach, the Germans were more alert. Fifty of Company G's 190 men were killed or wounded trying to get to the sea wall. In spite of the casualties, Dawson's outfit was still full of fight. The heavy-weapons men had their machine guns and mortars firing in no time. Protected by their fire, demolitions teams from each section blew a number of gaps through the barbed-wire barrier beyond the beach road.

By 7:30, Captain Dawson had led some of his men through the minefields on the ground between the road and the base of the bluffs. Some of the mines were fakes, but the men had to proceed cautiously just the same. They found one part of a safe route by stepping over the bodies of two soldiers from the first assault wave who had stepped in the wrong place, and had learned where mines were at the cost of their lives.

While the rest of Company G was catching up, Dawson and one man went on ahead looking for a good place to climb. The bluffs at this spot were sloping. They rose to 130 feet in a little more than two hundred yards. There was a shallow draw straight ahead, deep enough to provide some cover. Dawson thought that it looked like a good way up, unless it was mined. He and the man with him moved carefully, because the grass and clumps of brush made mines hard to see.

They were about halfway up the hill when a machine gun, shooting from somewhere near the top of the draw, stopped them. Neither man was hit, but the bullets had been terribly close. They wriggled back a few feet, out of the line of fire. Dawson thought things over. The machine gun was placed slightly below the top of the bluff and it controlled the whole upper half of the draw. If G Company was to use it, the machine gun would have to be knocked out.

Dawson sent his man back with a message for the company. "Keep coming," it said. "And stick to the draw."

Then Dawson, alone, started out to clear the way. He crawled far enough to the left to get out of the machine gunner's sight. Then he climbed up, hugging the ground, until he was higher than the gun position. He moved back to the right, approaching the emplacement from above and behind. He was within thirty feet of it before one of the three Germans manning the weapon spotted him and yelled a warning. While the Germans scrambled to swing the barrel around, Dawson pulled the safety ring on one of his fragmentation grenades.

He counted three, and lobbed it into the air with a stiff, straight arm. Then he buried his face in the ground for the longest moment in his life. The blast was followed by the whine of a hundred ricocheting splinters and a slight rain of dirt and pebbles. Finally Dawson lifted his head. His throw had been perfect. The gun and its gunners were silenced for good.

Now it was safe for his company to use the draw. By 8:30, nearly all of Company G had followed Dawson to the bluff top, and the sections were making ready to move ahead.

The route that Dawson had opened became a funnel for movement off that beach all the rest of the morning. Company G led the way for what, as the day wore on, became the deepest and most powerful advance off Omaha.

# CHAPTER SEVENTEEN

# THEY LED THE WAY

The Germans thought that the Omaha beach attack had been stopped, just as Rommel had ordered, at the water's edge.

The German officer in command of the guns at Pointe de la Percée could see the American dead and wounded lying on the sand. There were also ten tanks and a great many other vehicles burning. As far as he could make out, no one was advancing.

The center regiment of the German 352nd Division reported to its headquarters that, although it had taken heavy casualties from the naval shelling, it had stopped the landings.

Two Americans break down a door in Prum, Germany, with rifle butts. Middleton's VIII Corps took Prum on February 12, 1945.

At noon, German Army Headquarters was informed that the invasion had been completely smashed.

Hitler was about to appear at a reception near Salzburg for a new Hungarian prime minister when he got the news. He came into the room smiling. "It's begun at last," he announced.

Hitler was sure that the Atlantic Wall defenses were holding and that any small beachheads the Allies made would be wiped out within a week by German counterattacks.

Both the German communications and what they communicated were poor.

◦ ◦ ◦

For hours General Bradley, on board the *Augusta*, heard nothing except most disturbing reports from Omaha. Since dawn, he had been listening to scraps of information as they came over the navy's radio network. They had all been bad: messages about boats sunk, heavy enemy artillery fire, Ducks swamped, troops pinned down.

By 8:30, both the 116th and the 16th regiments should have been through the beach defenses and a mile beyond the bluffs to the highway that ran parallel to the coast through Colleville and Vierville.

The minutes ticked past. Eight-thirty came and went, and Corps had not even reported officially to Bradley that the landings had taken place.

Finally, at 9:45, Bradley got the first news from Corps: "Obstacles mined, progress slow . . . DD tanks . . . swamped." That was hardly reassuring. It did little except confirm the General's worst fears about the tanks. At noon, Bradley heard

General Dwight Eisenhower (right) and General Omar Bradley were instrumental in planning and executing the D-Day invasion.

The crew of a Duck changes its tire.

that the situation at the beach exits was "still critical." He was "shaken," to use his own word. He began to think about shifting the follow-up forces from Omaha to Utah and the British beaches where, he heard, the landings were going well. That would have been almost unthinkably hard. But the build-up of Allied strength ashore couldn't wait.

It was 1:30 before the General got a message that made him think the Omaha assault might succeed. "Troops formerly pinned down on the beaches . . . advancing up the heights behind the beaches," Corps reported.

The news, by the time it reached General Bradley, was really four hours old.

The delay was more than a matter of bad communications—although the arrangements to relay information from the beach to Corps and from Corps to Army had failed to work properly.

The main trouble was that the first advances, as we have seen, were made by small units, in many cases hidden in the smoke or in the grass on the bluffs. Many of the off-shore observers were watching only the five main beach exits, where almost no progress had been made. The men who got the Omaha assault moving again, after it had stalled, were all scattered in the spaces between the beach exits, or, in Moody's case, west of the westernmost draw.

The truth was that, by as early as nine o'clock, hundreds of men were advancing up the heights behind Omaha.

It was just hard, in the beginning, to spot them.

There were scores of others who, like Moody, Lambert, Schwartz, Bingham, Mullins, Shuford, and Dawson, had refused to stop trying.

Not all their names, by any means, are known. Not all of their actions were noticed or entered in the records.

But wherever an advance was made, the pattern was much the same. The movement started when one man (or in some cases, several men) took the first step. Nothing, broadly speaking, went according to plan. New decisions had to be made on the beach. Omaha succeeded because a few leaders showed the others that something could be done. They led, more often than not, by being themselves the first to make the move.

# CHAPTER EIGHTEEN

# THE TOEHOLD

The first small successes opened the way to larger advances.

On the extreme west of Omaha, where Moody had climbed the cliff, the Rangers found out that the fortified stone building was part of a maze of German positions with an involved network of trenches between them. It was one of the main Atlantic Wall strongpoints guarding the Vierville draw. The Rangers, helped by part of Company B of the 116th Regiment, attacked it again and again. It was late afternoon before they ended German resistance. But the strongpoint did fall at last and

An American soldier in one of the many hedgerows that crisscrossed Normandy.

all during the day it had been far too busy defending itself to add its share to the withering fire on the beach.

East of the Vierville draw, where Lambert had tried to blow the gap in the barbed wire, Company C of the 116th pushed on ahead from the top of the bluffs. Rangers, engineers, and men from five other companies joined in the advance. An assortment of parts of units can hardly be expected to fight with much precision or control. Yet by eleven o'clock, the column had moved inland a mile, swung to the right on the highway, and taken the town of Vierville.

At Les Moulins, where Bingham and Mullins had tried to get the assault moving, the Germans held onto the draw. But Major Bingham, with a small party of men from three different companies, had worked past the beach exit on its eastern side. With K, L, and I companies of the 116th, Bingham's group had moved about half a mile inland.

Captain Dawson's Company G of the 16th, after it got past the top of the bluff, moved quickly inland for a thousand yards, turned left, and fought its way through bitter German opposition toward the town of Colleville. The Germans counterattacked. Company G suffered twenty more casualties, which it could hardly afford. Like so many of the other groups on Omaha, Company G thought it was all alone except for the Germans. But as a matter of fact, a number of outfits were following in Company G's path. There were parts of four other 16th Regiment companies, and, by mid-afternoon, a battalion of the 18th Regiment, all backing up Company G.

Antilanding obstacles were scattered across Normandy's beaches.

By dark the Allies had a toehold in the Omaha beach sector. It was only a mile and half deep at its deepest, which was in the center, near Colleville. The right, around Vierville, was not joined up with the center. But the Vierville draw, now open, provided the troops with a supply route. All the leading units were short of vehicles, ammunition, and supplies. Only seven field artillery guns, including the Chief, were ashore, and there was an urgent need for more tanks and armored vehicles.

Omaha beach had cost a lot. Two thousand men were killed, wounded, or missing.

But most of five regiments were ashore, and in getting there, they had almost finished off the 352nd German Division. The crisis was past.

⦾　⦾　⦾

On all four of the other beaches the assault had gone far better.

The Utah beach attack had been remarkably successful. The 4th Division was ashore almost intact. Its casualties for the day were less than 200—thanks, in large part, to the job the paratroopers had done in the hours before dawn. Artillery shells were still falling on the beach itself, but the causeways from the beach were open and working. Two battalions of the 8th Regiment were six miles inland, guarding the highway to Cherbourg, and they had joined forces with one of the groups of paratroopers. There was still a great deal to be done. There was confusion because so many units were scattered, out of touch with one another, and unaware of what was happening any place except right where they were. But the beachhead itself—even though many of the commanders of the outfits on the ground didn't know it—was in excellent shape.

⦾　⦾　⦾

On Gold, Juno, and Sword, the British and Canadians had smashed through the Atlantic Wall and driven as much as seven miles inland.

At Le Hamel, on Gold beach, the British 50th Division found the German defenses strong and determined. But after the town of La Rivière, two and a half miles farther east, had been cleared, one German battalion broke and pulled out.

That left the road from La Rivière to the town of Bayeux, six miles inland, wide open. The Germans tried hard to plug the gap. But by the end of D-Day, the British had moved to within a mile of Bayeux, and had patrols on its outskirts, testing the strength of the defending troops in preparation for an attack at daybreak.

From Juno beach, the 3rd Canadian Division's advance had more than matched the effort toward Bayeux. The assault sections had pretty well worn themselves out in reducing the strongpoints at Courseulles. In one company, only twenty-seven men, including the company commander, survived the successful attack on the westernmost of the German fortifications. These included three pillboxes and twelve machine-gun nests. But the hard going on the beach had not stopped the division as a whole. When the day's fighting was done, the Canadians had moved from three to six miles beyond their beach, and one advance party—men of the North Nova Scotia Highlanders and the Sherbrooke Fusiliers—was ten miles inland, almost to the Caen-Bayeux highway.

Behind Sword beach, headed for Caen, the 3rd British Division had pushed forward four miles, just past a small town called Biéville. Most important, it had linked up with the bridgehead across the Orne that the paratroopers had seized during the night. It was only two miles short of Caen. And Caen, in German eyes, was a key to their defense of France. For the route from Caen to Paris, less than 150 miles ahead, was flat and open—and ideal for Allied tanks.

# ★ WAR BONDS ★

Much of the war's financing came through war bonds, and the War Finance Committee and War Advertising Council worked hard to encourage people to purchase them. By the end of the war, about 85 million Americans had done so.

The photo above shows a common type of purchasing drive: posters featuring female shipyard workers were widely distributed. Bond purchasers were allowed one vote for each bond they bought. Votes were counted and the woman who got the most votes was named "War Bond Girl." This Philadelphia contest was won by Kay McGinty, 4th row, 2nd column.

The photo opposite shows a special campaign: the public

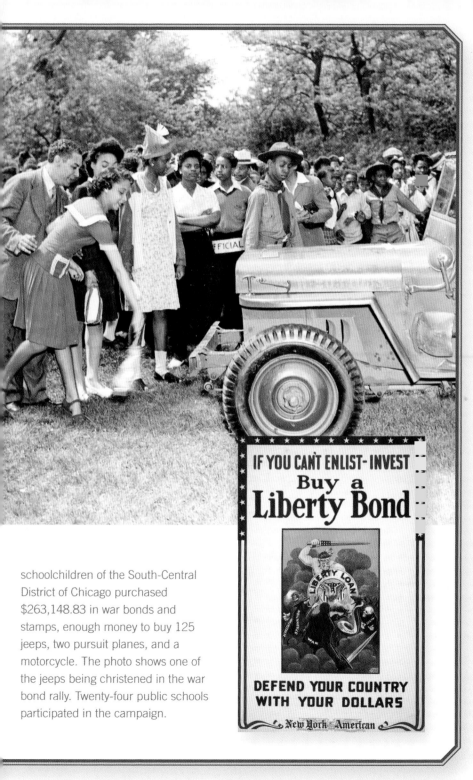

IF YOU CANT ENLIST–INVEST

Buy a
Liberty Bond

DEFEND YOUR COUNTRY
WITH YOUR DOLLARS

New York American

schoolchildren of the South-Central District of Chicago purchased $263,148.83 in war bonds and stamps, enough money to buy 125 jeeps, two pursuit planes, and a motorcycle. The photo shows one of the jeeps being christened in the war bond rally. Twenty-four public schools participated in the campaign.

· CHAPTER NINETEEN ·

# THE END HAD BEGUN

The greatest amphibious assault in the history of the world was a success.

Everywhere along the fifty-mile front, the assault sections had done what Hitler thought couldn't be done: They had smashed huge holes in the Atlantic Wall.

And through those holes, according to plan, poured the great weight of the invasion force.

It took eleven more months—from June 6, 1944, to May 8, 1945—for the Allies to bring the German war machine to its final defeat. But the D-Day victory had marked the beginning of that end.

Eisenhower (left) and Patton strategized the Allied advance into Germany.

By the end of the first week, the several D-Day penetrations had been joined together into one continuous beachhead.

Through the rest of June and most of July, the battle for Normandy raged, as the Allies slowly expanded their original toehold.

By July 25th, seven weeks from D-Day and a month after the capture of Cherbourg, the Allies had accumulated enough men, equipment, ammunition, and gasoline to break out of Normandy in a bold, powerful attack.

Once the movement started, it gained ground at an amazingly fast rate. In four days—August 19th to 23rd—the British and Americans trapped the German 7th Army between the towns of Falaise and Argentan, and tore it apart.

Our armored divisions, led by General George Patton, broke loose and swept across France faster than anyone, in his most optimistic frame of mind, had thought possible.

On August 24th, General Jacques LeClerc's Free French division entered Paris. These men had been fighting alongside the Allies in North Africa during the German occupation of France. With them, fittingly enough, was the American 4th Division—the men who had landed on D-day on Utah beach.

At the same time, a force of French and American troops, which had landed on August 15th on the southern coast of France, was in the process of capturing Marseilles, an important Mediterranean port. From there they were to move north, along the valley of the Rhone River, to join up with the main Allied armies.

By the second week of September, when the Allies formed a continuous line along the border between France and Germany itself, the rapid advance had to stop. It had gone much farther much faster than expected, and had outrun its supply lines. Before it could proceed, it was necessary for the Allies to capture a bigger port than Cherbourg and one closer to the fighting front.

So the British and Canadians, who had moved northeast from their sector into Belgium, attacked Antwerp, the largest port on the west coast of Europe. Despite desperate German resistance, it was in the Allies' possession, and being used, before the end of November.

But with the supply problem considerably eased, the weather turned against the Allies. Day after day the skies were gray and foggy so that the tactical air force couldn't see the ground well enough to give close support to the infantry attacks. The ground became, in many places, a sea of mud.

Weeks went by while the Allies waited for better weather and regrouped their forces for the next big offensive. This was to be the invasion of Germany itself. Allied divisions were massed in the north and in the south. That meant the Allies took a calculated risk. They left a weak spot in their line in the Ardennes Forest area.

That was where, on December 16th, after several days in which Allied aerial reconnaissance had been severely limited, the Germans counterattacked. Twenty-four German divisions hit a part of the front where the Americans had only four divisions. The deep dent they made in our lines gave the month-long battle its popular name, the Battle of the Bulge.

The fighting was savage. The losses on both sides were heavy. But by the time our lines were straightened out once more, the German army's power was greatly reduced.

By February, the Allies had resumed the offensive. By the end of March, the entire Allied front had moved across the Rhine, the last natural defensive barrier protecting the German heartland. In April, the armies on the Western Front took a million prisoners as they swept ahead into Germany. And the Russian armies, meanwhile, were moving west with almost equal speed.

On April 26th, forward elements of the Allied and Russian forces met at Torgau, some fifty miles north of Dresden, on the Elbe River.

On April 29th, the last of the German forces in Italy surrendered to the English and American troops there.

On April 30th, the Hamburg radio broadcast the news that Hitler was dead.

The highest ranking German admiral, Karl Doenitz, sent General Alfred Jodl and Admiral Hans-Georg von Friedeburg to SHAEF headquarters to give Germany's official surrender. General Eisenhower accepted it. The war in Europe ended at midnight on May 8, 1945. And, in the grand pattern of Allied strategy, it was then possible to turn the strength of all the nations to Japan's final defeat, which came on August 14th.

◦   ◦   ◦

It was for this, finally, that the first few men in their LCVPs had struggled onto the sands of Utah, Omaha, Gold, Juno, and Sword.

Only 335 days had elapsed between D-Day and the unconditional German surrender. Even in that short time, it had become difficult to remember back to the first hours after H-Hour, when no one had known, for sure, that the invasion would get ashore. Jubilation over victory, as was natural, crowded out the thoughts of dark, terrifying moments. Few cared to think, when victory came, about the moments when the assault sections on Omaha had stalled, and individual soldiers, of their own accord, had rescued the great assault.

But General Montgomery was confident that men would remember. He had made a prediction before D-Day. It had been included in a personal message to the assault troops which had been read to every man just as the invasion fleet had started across the English Channel.

"To us," Montgomery wrote, "is given the honor of striking a blow for freedom which will live in history; and in the better days that lie ahead, men will speak with pride of our doings."

# ★ D-DAY BY THE NUMBERS ★

The sheer number of troops and equipment involved in D-Day and the first few days of the invasion are almost impossible to imagine. Consider these numbers:

|  |  |
|---:|:---|
| **156,000** | Allied troops landed on first day. |
| **365,547** | Allied troops landed in first five days. |
| **4,413** | Allied soldiers died on D-day alone. |
| **4,000** to **9,000** | Germans were lost on D-Day. |
| **11,590** | aircraft were involved in, the invasion. |
| **14,674** | missions (sorties) were flown by Allied aircraft. |
| **6,939** | ships and boats were involved. |

**Left:** Omaha Beach near Colleville-sur-Mer, Normandy.
**Right:** Final dress rehearsal for "D-Day" Photograph shows American troops landing on beach in England during rehearsal for invasion of Nazi occupied France.

| | |
|---:|:---|
| **24** | warships were lost, plus 35 cargo ships and 120 landing boats. |
| **104,428** | tons of equipment landed on beaches on D-Day alone. |
| **16,000** | parachutists dropped in on the first day, in 925 troop planes. |
| **1,000,000** | gallons of gas were burned per day during first week of invasion. |
| **27** | war cemeteries in Europe hold |
| **110,000** | graves from all soldiers who fought in Europe on all sides |

# ★ CAST OF CHARACTERS ★

## ADOLF HITLER

Chancellor of Germany and supreme leader of German forces in World War II.

## WINSTON CHURCHILL

Prime Minister of Great Britain during World War II.

## FIELD MARSHALL BERNARD LAW MONTGOMERY

Commander of all Allied ground troops in Europe during World II.

## GENERAL OMAR BRADLEY

General of the Army for US forces in Europe during World War II.

## MAJOR SIDNEY V. BINGHAM JR.

Commander of F Company of 116th Regiment. Led the small party up a cliff off Omaha Beach, established the first breakthrough in enemy lines. Received Distinguished Service Cross.

## LIEUTENANT COLONEL THORTON L. MULLINS

Artillary field commander of 111th Field Artillery Battalion. Fearlessly directed artillery assault until killed in battle. Received Distinguished Service Cross.

## GENERAL
### DWIGHT D. EISENHOWER

Supreme commander of European forces in Europe during World War II, and later 34th President of the United States.

## FIELD MARSHAL
### GERD VON RUNDSTEDT

Supreme German Commander of Army during World War II

## LIEUTENANT
### WILLIAM D. MOODY

Officer in C Company of 2nd Ranger Battalion. Killed in battle, he was posthumously awarded the Distinguished Service Cross.

## PRIVATE
### INGRAM E. LAMBERT

Private in C-Company of 116 Regiment. Led assault on fortified fence. Although killed, his example inspired the rest of the company.

## CAPTAIN
### LOUIS A. SHULFORD

Commanding officer of C Battery. Managed to get one of 111th's howitzers ashore, establishing one of the first big guns brought into battle.

## CAPTAIN
### JOSEPH T. DAWSON

Commander of Company G, 16th Regiment. Led men off the beach and up the ravine to the top of a bluff, where he was wounded. Awarded Distinguished Service Cross.

# ★ TIMELINE ★

## 1939
SEPTEMBER 1
Germans invade
Poland, beginning
WW II.

## 1943
JANUARY
Churchill and
Roosevelt meet
in Casablanca to
discuss invasion
for liberating
France.

## 1944
JUNE 6
Liberation of
Europe begins
with invasion
at Normandy,
France by the
Allies.

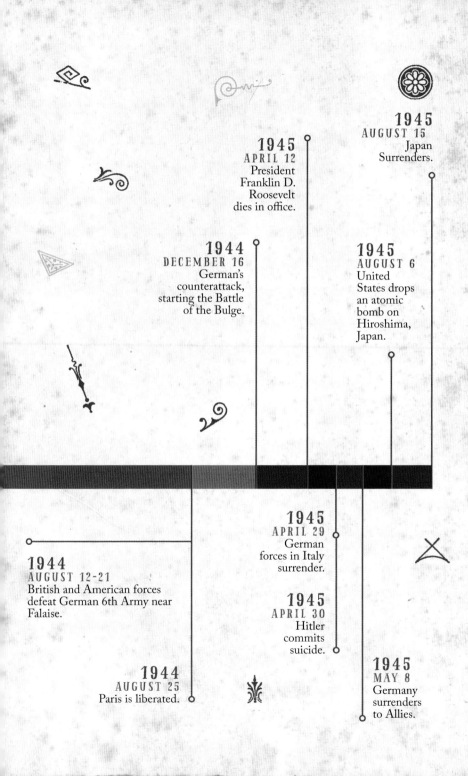

**1945**
AUGUST 15
Japan
Surrenders.

**1945**
APRIL 12
President
Franklin D.
Roosevelt
dies in office.

**1944**
DECEMBER 16
German's
counterattack,
starting the Battle
of the Bulge.

**1945**
AUGUST 6
United
States drops
an atomic
bomb on
Hiroshima,
Japan.

**1945**
APRIL 29
German
forces in Italy
surrender.

**1944**
AUGUST 12-21
British and American forces
defeat German 6th Army near
Falaise.

**1945**
APRIL 30
Hitler
commits
suicide.

**1944**
AUGUST 25
Paris is liberated.

**1945**
MAY 8
Germany
surrenders
to Allies.

# INDEX

## Image Credits

AP Images
25 (Berliner Verlag / Archiv / picture-alliance / dpa), 37, 41, 43, 47, 49 (US Army Signal Corps), 55, 56, 61, 65, 68, 69, 74, 75, 81, 82, 83, 93, 96, 99

Bridgeman Images
7, 137, 138

Getty Images
107 (Popperfoto), 108 (Bettman), 110 (Photo Quest)

Library of Congress
10 (Victor A. Lundy Archive), 11, 16, 31, 32, 91, 155, 156, 163 (Robert Capa), 164 (US Army Signal Corps)

National Archives
13, 21, 28, 33, 59, 60, 107, 108, 109, 110, 111, 117, 122, 123, 125, 131, 139, 143, 146, 147, 149, 152

Patton Museum
157

Shutterstock
87-88, 103, 109

# ABOUT THE AUTHOR

Bruce Bliven Jr. was a prolific writer of popular books and magazine articles on a broad range of subjects, from military campaigns to the history of the typewriter. Mr. Bliven began his career as a newspaper reporter, but later wrote for several national magazines, including *Life* and the *New Yorker*.

During World War II, he was a lieutenant in the 29th Division field artillery and took part in the D-Day landings in Normandy. Following the war, he resumed his writing career and eventually wrote more than a dozen books for adults and children, most of them on Unites States history. Mr. Bliven died at his home in Manhattan in 2002, at age 85.

An American soldier guards a group of German POWs.